Window of Time

By
Debra Hughey

Wake Forest, NC

www.scuppernongpress.com

Window of Time
Debra Hughey

©2025 Debra Hughey

First Printing

The Scuppernong Press
PO Box 1724
Wake Forest, NC 27588
www.scuppernongpress.com

Cover and book design by Frank B. Powell, III

All rights reserved. Printed in the United States of America.

No part of this book may be reproduced or transmitted in any form or by any means, electronic or mechanical, including photocopying, recording, or by any information and storage and retrieval system, without written permission from the editor and/or publisher.

International Standard Book Number ISBN 978-1-942806-79-0

Library of Congress Control Number: 2025921540

Table of Contents

Forward iii
Chapter One-Blue Sky Man Returns 1
Chapter Two-Spirit of the Past 7
Chapter Three-Apple Pie 11
Chapter Four-Dixieland 15
Chapter Five-Here They Come 19
Chapter Six-The Battles 23
Chapter Seven-Woodland Stew 27
Chapter Eight-Turtle of Stone 33
Chapter Nine-Stone Bridge 39
Chapter Ten-Tuckabatchee Town 47
Chapter Eleven-Unfriendly Welcome 53
Chapter Twelve-DeSoto 59
Chapter Thirteen-The Trader 63
Chapter Fourteen-Tuckabatchee 67
Chapter Fifteen-White Folks by the Thousands 73
Chapter Sixteen-Tecumseh 77
Chapter Seventeen-William Weatherford 83
Chapter Eighteen-Mims 87
Chapter Nineteen-The Horseshoe 93
Chapter Twenty-Rum with Sharp Knife 97
Chapter Twenty-One-Milly and Barent 101
Chapter Twenty-Two-Pole Cat Springs 105
Chapter Twenty-Three-Back Home Again 109
Epilogue 119

Forward

My daddy loved history and books, especially about Indians. I remember as a child, even before I could read, sitting in front of our big bookcase looking at pictures of Indian people. I was fascinated, then as now. As I got older, I had either a book or paper and pencil in hand. I knew one day I would write a book of my own — this will be number eight. Thanks to God for giving me the ability, and to my daddy for helping form my love of Native American History. Thank you to my sweet husband Randall for the loving encouragement and many, many hours of typing. Come with me now through the *Window of Time* and travel back into the past and experience history as it really happened.

Chapter One
Blue Sky Man Returns

I had noticed the morning sunlight shining through the upstairs window many times. It was just an old building, maybe one of the oldest in town and only the bottom floor was now being used. I was intrigued to see the light shine from one window across the room to the other. It was as if the light was time, and I had begun to call it the *Window of Time*. Alright, I said to myself, today is the day that I am going to ask for permission to go inside and look out that window. I know there is something special about that room and the window and I want to know what it is.

I knew the business owner and he had no problem with me going up to view the town from inside looking out. Just be careful on the steps, he had said, telling me also that it was a mess up there, that he had used the room for storage for many years.

For some silly reason, I was excited as I walked to the door that led to the stairs, the old boards squeaking as I stepped up. After climbing the ten or twelve steps, more than I had expected it would be, and more than slightly out of breath, I opened the door. Bright sunshine immediately welcomed me to the old room, dancing from window to window, just as I had hoped it would be. What a beautiful sight, I said to myself as I first glanced around the room. There was the usual assortment of things that had accumulated over the years and years of time, boxes stacked nearly to the ceiling, filled with who knows what. Piles of books lined one wall, and several old paintings were neatly stacked against another wall near the window.

I walked over to the window on the east side of the building, feeling the warm sunshine as it filtered inside. The view below was breathtaking. I had never seen the majestic river spanned by the long, long bridge and ruins of the old mill from that height and angle before and the old Confederate Armory stood as a sentinel of the past. Wow, I thought as I walked to the other side of the room to look out the opposite window, the one that had drawn me here. I could see for miles and miles, with the modern buildings blending with the ones that had been built long ago. This view too was spectacular. I was in no hurry to leave and had told the building owner that I might stay for a while. I walked back to the other side again and stood mesmerized as I looked upriver toward the smooth placid lake, almost a mile across as it slowly flowed up to the huge dam that had been built many, many years before on top of the natural bed of rocks that had been called, the great falls. The falls, still very obvious today as the water cascaded over the rocks before returning to the wild untamed river much as it had been decades and even eons ago. I stood quietly, watching the timeless flow of the river, wondering how much it had changed over time.

I heard a slight sound of movement behind me and thinking it was the owner of the building; I turned to ask him a question. To my surprise, and old man I had never seen before stood smiling at me. I caught my breath, thinking this must be a homeless person or some criminal hiding from the law and that I was in serious trouble.

"I knew you would come," the old man said smiling even broader. "What took you so long?"

"Who are you?" I asked, realizing that he was standing between me and the only door that led to the stairs.

"I am sorry. Didn't mean to scare you none. I don't mean no harm to you," he answered me.

Wondering if I should scream or bolt around him and get away as quickly as I could, I instead just looked at him, almost as if I was captivated by him. He was an old man, dressed in clothing from another time and his eyes were the bluest I had ever seen. There seemed to be something familiar about him.

"Who are you?" I asked again, my voice trembling. "Why are you here?"

"I know you have seen the sunlight dance from one of the windows," he pointed to the window facing the river, "to the other and you felt the pull to come up here. That's right ain't it?" The old man asked in a kind voice.

"Yes," I answered, relaxing a little. "I did. Please tell me who you are and how did you know that I had to come here? Your eyes," I could not help but saying. "I have never seen anyone with such blue eyes."

"Why, my name is Blue Sky Man," he said smiling again, "reckon you might have heard of me before."

I could not believe what he had said. Being familiar with the history of my town, I recognized the name immediately. "Blue Sky Man, sir" I stammered, "that is impossible! That person lived long ago in a different time."

"Yes, that is true, but I am Blue Sky Man. Please believe me." A sad look covered his face before he continued. "I am here for a special reason, you see, I'm here to take you on a journey."

"Sir, why would I go anywhere with you?" I asked, backing away from him and again fearing that I was in trouble. Maybe, I thought I had fallen asleep, and this was just a dream.

"I know this is hard for you to understand," the old man said gently, touching my arm. "Again, I say, I am Blue Sky Man and today I am just as real as you are. I know of the love you have for the people who made their homes on the banks of this beautiful river. I know you want to learn more about them," he paused. "Listen closely to what I am about to say. I am a time traveler. I can travel back in time and then return to the present. I can take you with me so that you may see firsthand the Creek people and the others and how they lived. You are the only one that I can take back. Will you come with me? Please."

"Sir, one or maybe both of us must be totally insane. This cannot be happening." I said as I began walking toward the stairwell door. "I think I need to leave now. It has been definitely interesting meeting you. Goodbye sir."

"No, don't go. Wait, please," the old man said, his voice cracking.

I turned back to look at him and froze. His wrinkled face was streaked with tears. I suddenly knew that the old man was telling the truth, that he thought that he was really a time traveler.

"Please let me explain," he said as I watched him slowly walk back to the window, with sunlight still dancing across the room. "As I told you, this is a special place and from here I can go back to a different time. Think the term folks use nowadays is portal or something like that. Now, I don't know nothing 'bout such things, but I tell you the truth, sure as my name is Blue Sky Man, I can go back, and you can go with me."

I was intrigued but still not believing him and thinking I would allow him to continue giving me his spill, but that I would escape when the chance arose. "Alright, Mr. Blue Sky Man," I said cautiously, "tell me more. If I go back with you, can I return to the present," I paused, "whenever I wish to? Will I be safe? Will I be harmed in any way? Can I interact with the people? Will they be able to see me? How long will I be gone? And once again, can I return home?" I asked quickly, watching his old face break out in a big smile.

"Yes, you most certainly can return home. All you need to do is tell me, "He smiled again, "but I do not think you will want to until our journey is complete. You will be safe, and no harm will come to you. At times they will see you and you will be able to talk with them, but then," he smiled again. "There will be times when they will not be aware of you. It is best that way. You will know when you can talk and when you should be silent. As far as how long we will be gone, I will have you back before the sun is directly overhead in the sky. Tell me when you are ready and I will take you on the most important journey you will ever make," Blue Sky Man said, smiling again, "this side of heaven, anyway."

Still planning to make my escape as quickly as I could, I took his outstretched hand. What in the world am I doing I thought.

"We will start slowly at first, then spiral back quickly. Close your eyes when I tell you to. Don't want you to get any of that motion sickness. We will go all the way back to about 950 A.D. What folks that study the Indians call the Woodland time period. We will stay mostly in this area, going no farther than a few miles from this spot. But there will be a few times when we will go a much farther distance away." He smiled at me again, "ready, then let's go," he said as he stretched his hand out to me.

Chapter Two
Spirit of the Past

The hand of Blue Sky Man was warm as I placed my trembling hand into his. Guess I have gone too far now to back out, I thought to myself and also saying a silent prayer that I wasn't setting myself up for some terrible misfortune.

"Now, remember Missy, don't be afraid. I promise you with my life again, that no harm will come to you. You will enjoy yourself much more if you will just relax and let the spirit of the past envelope you. Close your eyes for a moment and we will begin our journey back to a different time. I think you may recognize a few scenes in the beginning but remember to close your eyes tightly again when the big spiral begins."

Alright, we will see if this is real I thought as I opened my eyes expecting to see the room where I had stood and the sunlight dancing from window to window. "Oh, my goodness," I said out loud. Suddenly I was outside, standing on the street corner. People were walking on the sidewalk, laughing and talking, cars zipping up and down the street. I saw a red mustang and oh look, a canary yellow Camaro. I laughed seeing the puffy hair styles of the girls and the short, short skirts they were wearing. I remember wearing a few of those too. I looked at Blue Sky Man and smiled and noticed his bright blue eyes sparkle with happiness. Then suddenly the scene changed, I was in the same place, but no longer saw the red and yellow sports cars, but older ones like my daddy had driven. I saw a blue Pontiac and a brown paneled station wagon with white wall tires. Blue Sky Man nudged me on, and I began walking down the sidewalk beside older women dressed in longer, flowered dresses and some even had little hats perched on their tightly curled hair.

No one paid me any attention, so I thought they were not aware of me. Suddenly, I heard strands of *Jingle Bells*, and someone was singing "City Sidewalks, Busy Sidewalks, Dressed in Holiday Style." It must be Christmas I thought. On main street, as I walked with the crowd of shoppers with Blue Sky Man right by my side, I followed a rather plump lady into a clothing store. We listened as she chatted with the clerk, asking for a certain type of shirt for her husband's Christmas present. Then we turned the corner and went into a jewelry store filled with shinny necklaces and bracelets and beautiful rings. A man, wearing dungaree pants and a baseball cap picked out a lovely ruby ring with tiny diamonds on each side. He said he knew his wife would just love it. And I think he was right. I would love to have had one too.

Then I followed the crowd into another store that seemed to have just about everything including a large selection of toys. I watched with enjoyment as the children tugged on their mother's dresses asking for the toys they wanted from Santa. A boy, pointed to a red toy firetruck and a little girl, her eyes sparkling, picked out baby doll's all wrapped in blue and pink blankets.

Again, I followed the flow of people into other stores and realized this is just what I had done when I was a child. Out on the street again, I saw the big man himself, dressed in his red suit, his beard white and fluffy. I smiled again and to my surprise, Santa walked right up to me and handed me a red and white candy cane. "Merry Christmas," he said cheerfully and walked away toward a crowd of children. I looked at Blue Sky Man and he nodded, "Yes, he did see you."

In the blink of an eye, the scene changed, and I was with a large crowd of people standing in front of a huge several-floor building. They seemed to be celebrating something. A large stage, draped with red, white and blue banners, had been constructed in front of the building. The men and women were dressed in their Sunday best. I know now that I had gone back beyond the time of my birth. This was fascinating. Blue Sky Man smiled again, and I asked what the people were celebrating.

"Ask them yourself," he told me laughing.

"Can they see me?" I asked. He nodded his head. The people seemed to be all excited as they talked and laughed and all of them seemed to be friendly. I looked at a rather plump lady standing beside me and said, "excuse me mam, but what is the celebration all about?"

"Why, don't you know?" She answered me like I was joking with her.

"No Mam," I said politely. "I am just passing through and have just arrived here." I finished thinking quickly.

The lady smiled then and said, "Well, most of the people you see hear work for Grandma and,"

"Grandma," I said. "Who is Grandma?"

The lady laughed, "Why Grandma, that's what we a call the cotton mill. You see, the mill company pretty much takes care of all of our needs. We all have worked real hard making the cloth the government folks use for the war needs. Now mind you, many young men have been across the big water fighting them Germans." She paused, looking sad, "and some of them didn't make it back home. But today we are being honored for doing such good work. Think some of the men up on that big stage are going to do some talking and brag on us. Hope they don't go too long. Heard we all gonna have some cake and such."

"Thank you, mam, I hope you all have a nice time today," I said kindly as Blue Sky Man touched my arm, and I knew it was time to move on to a different time. Just before this happened, I heard the slow drone of the motor of a low-flying airplane. I looked puzzled at the old man beside me.

He smiled; his blue eyes again sparkled with humor. "Time," he said, "that's the sound of time."

Before I could ask what he meant by that, we were standing beside a sandy dirt street, and I knew we had moved on with our journey.

Business Day
Street Scene of Tallassee Around 1915

Business Day in Tallassee, Alabama, in 1915 as it was in all rural communities, was Saturday. The Bank of Tallassee was chartered August 29, 1913, and was located on North Anti Street. On December 3, 1914, The Bank of Tallassee purchased the Peoples Savings Bank & associates, and with building. The Bank of Tallassee then moved from North Anti Street unto the Peoples Savings Bank Building, which then became The Bank of Tallassee Building, located on the southeast corner of North Ann Street and Barnett Boulevard. The building was renovated after a fire in the late 1930's, was renovated again in 1951, at which time The Flesh's Drug Store area (formerly Bilbrey's Optical) became part of the Bank. The building suffered fire damage again in the late 1950's. Restoration was done, and The Bank of Tallassee operated at this location until May, 1965, when it removed to its present location, 304 Barnett Boulevard.

Life in the early 1900's was not so complicated, and most problems could be worked out between the people as reflected by the trade Mary Ann has just made for a mixed string of fish with only one walleye.

Presented by The Bank of Tallassee in observance of its 80th anniversary - August 29, 1993

1915 Business Day in Tallassee.

Window of Time

Chapter Three
Apple Pie

There were no cars, only wagons and buggies being pulled by big black or gray horses. The men wore overalls and straw hats, and the women's dresses were long, almost touching their black boots. Some of them had shawls draped over their shoulders and colorful bonnets covered their heads.

I looked at Blue Sky Man and asked, "about nineteen hundred?"

He laughed, "You're pretty good," he said, "1920."

I stood and watched in amazement at the goings on around me, the bright sunlight dancing all around. The people all seemed to be happy, the men and women greeting each other with hellos and big smiles and the children were joyfully running ahead of the wagons. Most women had big pretty baskets filled with fruits and vegetables just picked from their gardens. A few had freshly baked bread and pies that looked delicious. Some of the men had strings of fish, catfish and bass, walleye just caught from the river earlier that morning. Others had various leather items like bridles and bits that had been meticulously made in their barns.

This must be some sort of trade day I thought, and I bet it is Saturday. I was so intent in watching the scene before me that I accidentally bumped into an older lady with her pie-filled basket clutched tightly in her hands. She abruptly turned around, I think to reprimand me, but instead she just stood and stared at me.

"Oh, excuse me mam," I said. "I wasn't watching where I was going."

"You ain't from around here, are you?" She asked, looking up one side of me and then the other.

"No mam," I answered, remembering what I had said earlier, "I'm just passing through."

"Never seen a lady," she paused, "You are a lady ain't you? Wearing such cloths like you got on."

I looked down at my slim-fit jeans and bright blue T-shirt, thinking that I did look out of place. "Yes mam, I do consider myself a lady, this is uh, the style where I come from," I answered, smiling.

"And where is that pray tell?" The woman asked with a little sarcasm in her voice.

How do I answer that I thought, looking over at Blue Sky Man who stood to the side smiling. "Oh, pay her clothing no mind mam," he said. "She's with me and I do need to get her some proper cloths. I'll see to that directly. Tell me mam, what sort of pies you got there? They sure look mighty good," Blue Sky Man said as he turned to me and winked.

The lady smiled at the compliment and cheerfully answered, seeming to have forgotten how I was dressed. "Well, I got some apple and some pear too. Now, where did you say you all are from?"

Blue Sky Man smiled again, his blue eyes sparkling in both amusement and mischief. "Well mam," he replied. "You see, we are just traveling through time, never staying any place for long, but my young friend here has family close by."

"Did you say traveling through time?" She asked, her forehead wrinkling in a frown. "What in tarnation do you mean by that?"

"Oh Mam, I just got my words all confused. I meant to say, taking our time traveling." Changing the conversation quickly, he continued, "So how much for one of your pies? I am hungry and I just know your pies are delicious." Blue Sky Man looked at me and smiled.

"Well sir, I think I understand now. How 'bout fifty cents? Which kind would you like?" The lady asked, pulling the colorful cloth away from the pies.

"I'm a little partial to apple pies, so I think I would like apple." Blue Sky Man answered, reaching into his pocket for two quarters. "Now mam, if you have time, me and my friend here would enjoy it very much if you could quick like tell us what some of these buildings are called. They are mighty big for such a little town."

"Oh, I would be happy to and please forgive me for being so rude. My name is Mabel, Mabel McKenzie. Why, my family have lived here for generations, even back to the time when them injuns was here." She sat her basket down and pointed to a big white building on the hill overlooking the river. "That's called the white store, and it's used for all sorts of things. That's the bank building over there and," pointing to the other side of the dusty street, "those big stone buildings and the stone came from the riverbank. They are called the Company Store buildings. But why do you all want to know this?"

"Oh, just curious," Blue Sky Man said, laughing, "think its about time we mosed along. Thank you, mam." He said, taking my arm and I knew it was time to move on again.

"Ready?" He asked

I nodded in excitement.

"This has been just the beginning. I wanted you to know that my time travel is real. Now we're going to a different time. I want you to close your eyes now." He squeezed my arm reassuringly. "Here we go!"

Chapter Four
"Dixieland"

Feeling a little unsteady, I opened my eyes again. I was standing on the same dusty street corner that I had been on a few seconds ago, but my surroundings were very different. There were fewer of the stone buildings and not as many people as before. Somewhat, old rickety wagons were drawn by slow, prodding mules. Most of the men had full beards and the women wore homespun dresses that nearly dragged the ground. I was trying to decide what time period that I was in when suddenly a young man came racing down the street nearly running me over. He was excited and yelling words that I did not understand.

"Oh, 'cuse me mam," he said. "Have you heard the news?"

I shook my head. "No, what is all the excitement about?"

"Why, mam, Alabama has pulled out, we have seceded from the Union." The young man answered as he continued to run down the street proclaiming the news.

"January 11," I said out loud.

Blue Sky Man smiled, "I figured that you would know that right off. Come with me before we go any further. Spec the women folks will start throwing rocks at you if we do not get you some different clothes. "Come on," he said as we walked on down the dusty street, stopping at a neat little clapboard house surrounded by flowers.

We walked up to the house as if we were going to visit an old friend. Blue Sky Man winked at me as he knocked on the door. An older woman, her hair pulled neatly back in a bun, wearing a plain blue high-neck dress with a flowered apron opened the door. Looking a little confused, she quickly regained her composure. He Southern manners taking over, she smiled politely, "may I help you folks with something?"

"Yes mam, you can," Blue Sky Man answered, again using the same wording that he had used earlier. "You see, me and my friend here are, uh are doing some traveling around and my friend is not dressed for uh, the places were going." He smiled again, "and we were wondering, uh if you might have an old dress that you could spare for my friend. 'Course I will pay for it and mam we are a little hungry. We would appreciate any food you have; anything would be fine." He paused, "Oh mam, I am sorry, please let me introduce myself. My name is Blue Sky Man and this is, uh Missy." I did not know if he knew my name and had just quickly given a name that came to him.

I smiled at him and then to the lady in front of us, thinking I needed to speak to her as well. Our appearance must have been shocking to her. "Yes mam, I would really appreciate a dress just like you are wearing. What I have on is uh, not quite right. And mam," I continued, trying to convince her that we meant no harm. "Mam, did you hear the news, that Alabama has seceded from the Union?"

"What! No, I did not know that" she answered. "When? I am both happy and sad to hear that. But, yes please come on inside. You do look like nice folks, and I think I can find you a dress. I used to be 'bout your size and," looking more closely at me, she smiled, "you do need a dress. Where did you get those cloths, you are wearing anyway?"

Forgetting that I was not in the 21st century anymore, I almost said Belks but stopped myself. "Oh, I do not remember but I sure would be more comfortable in a dress." I replied quickly.

The nice lady smiled as she looked me over once again. "I am sure you will. You all know I just cooked up some cornbread and I have fresh-churned butter. Would you like to share dinner with me. Then we will find you a suitable dress." Looking down at my feet, she frowned, "and some shoes. Honey Child, you will not be able to walk very far in whatever you call those things on your feet!"

I looked down at my sandals that I had just bought and had paid way too much for. I could not help laughing. "You know mam, you are right, and I would appreciate some good walking shoes. I think my friend, Blue Sky and I have a long ways to walk."

    Blue Sky Man and me stayed a long while with the nice lady, whose name we found out was Mary Walker, enjoying the cornbread and butter she had shared with us. We talked about the news of succession that we had just heard. Our new friend, with tears running down her face, explained the reason for her sorrow. My father, she had said, fought in the war in the last century. The war that gave us freedom from that big country across the water. She had paused in reflection and continued, but you know that freedom gave us the right to live like we want, and we do not need them folks form up north telling us what to do neither. She had paused, you all do not reckon that there will be any fighting, do you? She told us her husband had long-since passed away, but she did have two sons that lived on down the road aways and that they had five sons that she knew would take up their old squirrel guns and fight.

    Meanwhile, just outside, men and boys were firing their guns into the air and shouting in jubilation, "away, away down south in Dixie." Blue Sky and me looked at each other in sadness. We both knew what lay ahead for Dixie Land.

    Miss Mary took my hand and told me to follow her, and she would find me some suitable clothes. We walked into the small, neat bedroom which smelled of lilac. She quickly found me a dress much like the one she was wearing except in a lovely shade of pink. She laughed and said it was just a little small for her. I had laughed too, thinking it was probably more than a little small for the now plump lady. The shoes, on the other hand, lacked much to be desired, but they did fit me. I quickly changed, putting my jeans and sandals in a cloth bag, knowing that I would certainly look out of place when I returned to my time.

    Blue Sky smiled at me, "that will do right nice," and said, "I think it is time for us to move on back now."

    "What do you say?" Miss Mary asked, "move on back?"

    Blue Sky Man smiled again, his brilliant blue eyes sparkling, realizing he had almost said something that might give us away.

"Oh yes, we need to move on back outside and continue on our journey. Miss Mary, it has been most delightful meeting you and I thank you so much for the clothing and food. Do not think I have ever had cornbread that good. Now, please tell me what do I owe you?"

"Mr. Blue Sky Man," Miss Mary said, her own eyes shining with happiness. "It had been my pleasure to meet both of you. This has been so nice, and you do not owe me a cent. If you ever are back this way, please stop in and see me. Maybe I could fry up some chicken for you."

I hugged the nice old lady and thanked her again, "Miss Mary, I feel like a Southern Bell now." Thinking of what was ahead, I added, "Please take care."

With that Blue Sky took my arm and we were again standing out in the street hearing the shouts of *Dixie* — Dixieland.

Chapter Five
Here They Come

Seconds later, we were standing back up the dusty street and watched as men and boys, some riding horses, most walking and many coming from far away, all gather under a large oak tree. I turned to Blue Sky Man and asked him what was happening.

"Its July 1861 and these fellows are signing up to go and do their part in the war. This is the 13th Alabama Infantry Regiment. They will become part of the Army of Northern Virginia. They will fight in many of the big battles and many of these men will not return home." Blue Sky paused, "including a grandson of the nice lady, Miss Mary. Another of her grandsons will be badly wounded and will walk with a limp for the rest of his life,"

I sadly watched the jubilant men line up to sign papers that would change the lives, in some way, of all of them. "I wish we could tell them what lies ahead," I said, fighting back tears and remembering I myself had many distant family members who had proudly fought in the war.

"Me too," Blue Sky Man answered. "But we can only go back to the past. We cannot change anything. Come," he said, taking my arm, "there is much more to see."

Blue Sky Man led me to a beautiful grass-covered spot between two tall pine trees on a hillside. The view below us was spectacular. On the bank of the rapidly flowing river stood the majestic stone mills, known as the Falls Manufacturing Company. Just above, the water poured over the natural falls that harnessed the energy for the mills. I was amazed that men of this time period were so creative and how in my time period, nothing could be done without a computer.

As we watched the busy mill activity going on below us, Blue Sky Man and I talked about the sad things that were soon to occur. Being very interested in history, I was pretty well versed in the events of the Civil War, or the War for Southern Independence, but was totally heart-broken by what Blue Sky

Man told me.

"Missy, Blue Sky Man said, smiling, "it is alright if I continue to call you by that name, ain't it?" I nodded. I do know your name, shoot, I know all about you, that's why I chose you to come on this journey with me back in time."

"You do?" I asked surprised.

"Yes, I do, and the reason will be revealed to you later. Now, to save time," Blue Sky Man laughed at the reference he had made about time, he continued, "I need to tell you about some of the sad, hard times the people of your town will have to endure.

'Course, you know that folks were all excited in the beginning. All the older boys and men couldn't wait to join up. We saw that happen. Now, all southern men knew about shooting guns and fighting but it still took a little training to do this in a group. The women got busy, making the things they could for their men folks. Soon word came it was time to join up with groups from other towns to form the Confederate Army, or the Rebel Army as they called themselves. He paused, smiling, "all was good, this little war wouldn't last long, why the Rebels would go out and take care of them Yankees right quick like. The women folks-the mamas, the wives and sweethearts, all lined the streets waving handkerchiefs and shouting words of endearment to their men as they passed by.

Then, they were gone, dust from their horses still floating in the summer air. First one then another gasped as they realized what this meant. They had just watched the ones they loved march off to war…to war. Tears streaked down their faces as they turned, taking the hands of their small children as they walked back down the dusty street to their empty homes."

Blue Sky Man became silent for a minute before he continued on, "you know that must have been real hard on those women. Oh, they were strong, hard-working women, but now they were all on their own. Oh, they made out alright for awhile then the crops came in and the animals had to be seen to. One of the children took sick and the doctor had joined along with

the others too. Many began to have feelings of despair. Then the ultimate happened, the old telegraph operator sadly took down the message that came over the wire. One of the local boys had taken a bullet to the chest. His last word had been Mama.
The war that had supposed to have been quickly over was now in the third year. Supplies were scant, food even more so. The soldiers had had very little to eat, and many nights went to sleep on their thin blankets, hungry. Their shoes had long since worn out, their feet blue with cold." Blue Sky Man stopped, wiping a tear from his wrinkled old face. "The field hospital had no room for all the injured and not enough doctors to tend to the wounded, mangled soldiers from the southland." He paused again, "Missy, I saw too much. I cannot bring myself to take you there. Many, many of the brave Rebel soldiers valiantly gave their all."

Neither of us spoke, Blue Sky Man seeing the horrors of war still vivid in his mind and I just wanted to go somewhere and hide myself from what I had just heard.

After a few minutes, the old man lifted his head and smiled at me. "Please forgive me. I am usually stronger than this. Reckon, I'm just getting old," laughing he continued, "I do want you to experience and see for yourself the war. Come take my arm and close your eyes. Don't open them until I tell you. We will be actually moving away from this site here now. One more thing, do not be afraid.

Some folks have asked if any battles actually occurred in this area. Well, yes there were a couple. I reckon you could call them skirmishes. If you remember," Blue Sky Man smiled at me. I was becoming fond of the smile that lit up his old, wrinkled face, "and I am sure you do, but in June of 1864, the Confederate leaders decided to start making the rifles or carbines, as they called them, here at the mill that was built in 1844. Well, now you also know that the Yankees came down south and destroyed and burned houses, bridges, train tracks and anything else they found." He laughed, "Missy, you know them Yankees, why they were just plain mean! They had learned that the carbines, and they were mighty fine guns too, were being made here, so here they come."

Chapter Six
The Battles

"Now Missy, if I remember right, a fancy general by the name of Rousseau sent a Major Baird to do some Yankee destruction here. Following the train track, they ended up down at a place called Chehaw Station. I know you have been there before, but now its July 1864," Blue Sky finished with a sad expression covering his face.

Before I opened my eyes, I could smell the smoke and hear the rapid repeat of rifles being fired. I could hear men yelling and realized that what I heard was the Rebel Yell that I had been told about so many times. What a sensational sound I thought, then remembered that I was standing very near an actual battle. Do not be afraid, I told myself. Do not be afraid.

I saw many soldiers dressed in blue charging a much fewer number of men, their tattered uniforms in gray. I slid behind a bush, not knowing if I could be seen and noticed that Blue Sky Man was there too. He had said that I would face fear. He was definitely right about that. He whispered to me to be still.

"These fellows here are the local home guard, but help is on the way," he said softly and smiled when we heard the melancholy sound of the whistle as the train rumbled down the track. The track the Yankees had come to take apart. We watched when a small battalion of teenage boys jumped from the train, not waiting for it to completely stop. Waving their hats and flintlock muskets in the air, they joined the home guard with renewed energy. I looked at Blue Sky Man and whispered, "who? They look like children."

"Yes, but they can fight, most as good as any and ready to kill 'em some Yankees, they are," he answered me. "They are cadets from the University of Alabama. Maybe 16 or 17 years old. They been in training over there in Selma."

It seemed like the fighting began to intensify. As I stood watching in amazement, suddenly a cadet fell at my feet. I looked down in horror as bright red quickly covered his gray shirt sleeve. He looked at me in fear and softly said. "Help me."

I looked at Blue Sky Man, silently employing him to tell me what to do. "You know," he answered.

I remember from watching westerns on TV that the blood flow should be quickly stopped. I pulled up my dress and tore a strip from my borrowed slip and tightly wrapped it around the young man's arm. Blue Sky Man looked at me and nodded and took my hand. "Thank we have gotten a little too close. We need to back away."

Then, coming from the other direction, a group of militia arrived to help the home guard and cadets. Soon after the soldiers in blue began backing away in with drawl. In only seconds, Blue Sky Man and me were standing on a hillside as the battle seemed to end and each side gathered their wounded and dead. The Yankees claimed the victory, saying that forty Confederates had been killed, but the actual number had been only six.

I looked at Blue Sky Man, still shaking from the event that I had just witnessed. "What about the boy, did he live?" I asked with tears forming in my eyes.

"Yes, he did," Blue Sky Man smiled. "He thinks you saved his life, and you did." Laughing, he continued, "no one could figure out where the cloth tourniquet came from. They thought the poor lad was delirious when he told them a nice lady had held his hand and tied the bandage around his arm."

"You said there were two skirmishes, are we going to see the second?" I asked.

"No, you have seen enough. A big battle would be too much for you to bare. I will tell you about it now and then we will move on. There is so much for you to see," Blue Sky Man cleared his throat and began. "The second local skirmish was known as the Battle of Franklin, and the war was nearly over when it took place. April 15, 1865, it was. You remember that the armory here had been making the carbines for the Rebel soldiers to use, and the officers sure didn't want them Yankees to get a hold of 'em. So, it was decided to move the guns some where's else."

"Where?" I asked curiously.

Blue Sky Man laughed, "Well, I know most everything I reckon, but I'll be darn if I know where them guns are. You see, it's a mystery of sorts. It has been said by some that the carbines were put on a train and all 500 of 'em were shipped to Macon, Georgia. Others say they were packed in boxes and hid somewhere near the armory, maybe in a tunnel or even concealed in one of the walls in the mill building. Still others claim that they were just dumped in the river, thinking it best to destroy them so the Yankees couldn't get 'em. I do know that a few of them were not destroyed or hidden. It was said that some of them did end up in the hands of the Yankee officers, maybe as souvenirs. And 3 or 4 have showed up over the years in museums." Blue Sky Man paused to catch his breath and continued. "Now back to the second skirmish at Franklin, don't get confused with that big battle that happened up in Tennessee. A General Wilson was the Yankee leader, and he sent some of his soldier ahead to burn every bridge and mill along the Tallapoosa River. Now you know the Tallapoosee had many twists and bends," he smiled again. "Most like a big ole snake it is. Well, anyway, them soldiers, they got on the wrong side somehow. Don't think they had a very good sense of direction, and they also had an old map. So, when they saw an old man of color, they asked him to lead them to the mill on the river. He told them they would have to cross the river back to the other side to get to the mill. The Yankee commander just figured the old fellow was lying and so they shot him, think they shot him dead. The Yankee troops stayed on the east side of the river and were met head on by a bunch of the local home guard and militia. So, they then hightailed themselves on up the road, never ever seeing the armory mill. So, that's how the armory here came to be the only Confederate Armory not destroyed in the war."

"What an amazing story," I said. "Has anyone ever searched for the carbines?"

"Oh yeah, many have speculated that they were here or

there or some place else entirely over the years, but other than the few I mentioned, they have never been found. And I have a feeling that they never will," Blue Sky Man smiled at me again and touched my arm. "Ready to move on?" He asked. "We're going way back now and then work our way forward again. Do not open your eyes. Here we go."

Chapter Seven
Woodland Stew

Before I opened my eyes, I realized that I was in a different place. I could hear the sound of running water, so I knew the river was nearby. I heard the redbird and the wren cheerfully calling their mate. I could smell meat of some sort cooking over and open fire. I could hear garbled voices in the distance, but I could not understand the words. I slowly opened my eyes, fighting the dizzy feeling that overwhelmed me.

Blue Sky Man, still holding my hand, softly said, "Be still, this will soon pass, and you will be fine. We will remain out of sight for a little while. We do not need to reveal ourselves just yet. When we do, remain silent. Let me do the talking. You will not understand what is being said and you will again face fear," he paused. "Do not worry, if I see that you are in any real danger, I will take your hand, and we will go from this place and time."

"Where are we and what time period is this?" I asked with knots beginning to form in my stomach.

Blue Sky Man smiled, "My dear, we are in a place where you have wanted to see for a long time. You are not very far from home. Not sure what the actual date is, but it is spring in the year 950 A.D."

"You mean we are in the time period called Woodland?" I asked in disbelief, my voice quivering with anticipation and also fear.

Blue Sky Man nodded his head, I am going on ahead and check out the mood of the people that you will soon see. I am almost certain there will not be a problem, but I do need to make sure. They ain't ever seen anyone who looks like you before. Wish I had a deerskin shirt and skirt for you," he smiled, "I'll see what I can do about that too."

"Wait," I employed, "What about you?"

He smiled again, "Oh, been here before, several times. They know me, can even talk to 'em some. Got a mighty strange way of talking though."

Blue Sky Man parted the bushes and walked the worn path to the small camp of people. I remained very still, not daring to move. I didn't think it would be a good thing if they found me before Blue Sky Man explained my appearance here. What was he going to tell them anyway I wondered. I was actually going to see Woodland people, I thought, trying to quell my fear with excitement.

Soon I could hear Blue Sky Man being greeted by several men and women. They seemed happy to see him, but I had no idea what they were saying to him. It wasn't long before Blue Sky Man returned with a bundle of deerskin under his arm. "Got you a dress and some moccasins," he said happily.

"What did you say about me?" I asked.

"Oh, just that you were my friend from a long, long walk away." He laughed. "I told them that you wanted to meet them. Here, go behind that other bush and change into the clothing of the Woodland time period. Put your dress in this," he ordered, handing me a deerskin bag. "You will need it again on our way back.

When a came out from behind the bush, Blue Sky Man nodded his head in approval. "With your skin complexion, you don't look a whole lot different from their women," he smiled. "Sept for your blue eyes and light hair. Guess we got that in common. Come on. Just smile, even if you said anything, they wouldn't understand," he said, taking my hand.

I took a deep breath and followed Blue Sky Man up the path into a clearing. I stopped in amazement, realizing that I had indeed stepped back a long way in time. In front of me, were a group of about twenty-five or thirty actual Woodland people. I had read many books about the Woodland time period, so I was not too surprised at the scene before me. They were a little darker complected than I thought, and the men were a little taller. The women were shorter, and both had long almost black hair, some of which was pulled back and tied with a leather cord. Eyes of striking pools of black stared back at me with fear and amazement. They were speaking in almost guttural tones among themselves. A small child, I couldn't tell if it was a boy or a girl, reached out to touch my arm, which was quickly pulled back by its mother.

    I remembered what Blue Sky Man had told me to do, so I took a deep breath and smiled. None of them moved. They stood staring at me as if I planned to harm them in some way. I realized they were more afraid of me than I was of them. I noticed that most of the men were wearing only breech cloths, some had on some sort of skin leggings, but still no shirt. The women wore shirts and skirts made of deer hide and few of them were wearing no shirt at all! I was very happy that I had a shirt to wear. I smiled again at that thought. My eyes moved to the surrounding area. This seemed to be only a small camp, a fishing or hunting camp maybe right here by the river. I knew that in the Woodland time period, villages were becoming larger with many more people. I knew too that this site was not suitable for a large village. There must be a larger village close by, I thought. There were several hide-covered frame structures that I recognized as houses. Each one had a fire pit in front of it with meat sizzling on forked sticks. The aroma made me realize how hungry I was. Sure, hope Blue Sky Man can get us an invite for supper, I thought. Blue Sky Man, where was he? I didn't see him anywhere. I began to panic. Then, I saw him standing on the edge of the group of Woodland people. He was talking to an older woman. She was very pretty and looked at him sadly. I was surprised to see him lift her chin and kiss her. Oh, my goodness I thought! He said he had been here before. She must be his woman. He looked up at me and smiled then walked toward me.

    "I call her Fawn Woman," he said, "Have many sweet friends in many places in time. So, are they what you expected them to be?" He asked, looking out at the group in front of us, who still stared at me like I had horns or something.

    "Pretty close to what I thought," I replied, wishing I could help them to understand that I was not here to harm them in anyway and that I was just as curious about them.

"Hungry, ain't you?" He asked.

I nodded, still smelling the meat cooking over the fire. Blue Sky Man said something to them and pointed to me. One of the men, who seemed to be the leader nodded and turned to the woman beside him. To my surprise she looked at me and smiled.

Blue Sky Man turned to me and said, "Well then, let's go eat."

He took my hand and led me to one of the skin houses and we sat down on a big log. The Woodland woman then handed me a pretty pottery bowl and a spoon made of wood. I watched in awe as she filled it with a dark stew-like substance and then turned to the fire and with a stone knife cut meat from the forked sticks. I was shaking with excitement. I was about to eat a meal prepared by a Woodland woman. Oh my, I thought how could this be. The woman said a few words in her language, wait, I thought. What is their language? What do they call themselves? I wanted to know this but how could I.

Blue Sky Man smiled at me again. "She said that the stew is hot and I might add that you never have tasted anything like this before. Be prepared."

I smiled and noticed that all the Woodland people had gathered around to watch me and see the reaction I would have to their food. I wondered if this might be a test of sorts. Suddenly, I wasn't hungry after all. What in the world was in this, this stew or whatever it was. Maybe I should try the meat first, but what kind of an animal was this? I knew for sure that it wasn't beef steak!

Blue Sky Man took his bowl and meat from the woman and immediately began to eat. He motioned for me to do the same. I took a deep breath. Here goes I thought. Hope I don't throw up. I took a small bite of the meat. It was a little tough and had a strong taste, but it was definitely something that I could eat. Then I picked up the spoon, which was neatly carved with designs. Pretty, I thought. Maybe I can take this back with me. I knew I was putting off the inevitable. Every eye was on me, even the children stood motionless as I dipped the spoon into the bowl and then lifted it to my mouth. Can't stop now, I thought, here goes. Oh my, what is this? It was horrible. At first, I had the strong desire to spit it out, but then the strange flavor seemed to change entirely and tasted quite similar to stew like I had bought at the grocery store. Having forgotten that I had been watched, I was startled when the Woodland people around me began laughing and yelling. I guess this is a good thing I thought and took another bite of meat and then more of the stuff in the bowl.

Blue Sky Man smiled at me. "You did it!"

"What did I do?" I asked. "I was hungry, so I ate." I answered, wiping my mouth with my hand.

"You have been accepted by the people," Blue Sky Man said happily. "If you had not eaten their food, well, we probably would have had to leave this place. But now, we can stay for a while if you would like."

Rock Park Creek which flows into the Tallapoosa River. Was a likely Woodland Village site.

Chapter Eight
Turtle of Stone

While the people, and I learned that's what they call themselves, still watched me closely, they did not seem to be as frightened of me. I found that humorous. They did not know that I was actually frightened out of my wits. Blue Sky Man told me that there was a much larger village on the other side of the hill. And this, as I had thought, was a fishing or hunting camp of sorts. This group liked being on their own and might stay here or move on down the river. Blue Sky Man told me that I was completely safe and could wander around and see how they lived. He thought I could learn a lot that way and he would answer questions later.

"What are you going to do?" I asked, afraid that he was going to leave me here.

He smiled his usual beautiful smile and spoke. "Well Missy, I got a little catching up to do with Fawn Woman. I'll be back directly." With that he turned and disappeared into the group of Woodland people.

I had finished my meal of whatever it was and handed the woman my pottery bowl, I had actually eaten out of a pottery bowl made by a Woodland woman, oh my goodness! I would have loved to have kept the wooden spoon but gave that back as well. I didn't think they would take too kindly of me for taking the spoon, which must have taken a long time to make.

The woman smiled at me and looked a little confused. I guess she didn't know what to do with me now. I made the motion of washing my hands. She smiled and motioned for me to follow. She took me to a little rocky branch that ran into the river where I kneeled and washed my hands and mouth. The food had been more than a little greasy. I stood and looked at the river, oh how different it looked. I wonder if they call it Tallapoosa.

"Tal-la-poo-sa," I said and pointed to a much smaller river than I was used to seeing.

"Tal-la-poo-see," she answered me. I had no idea if the Woodlan people already called the river by that name. Then I remembered that the old name for the river was Little Rocks, but at least we had communicated.

I looked up the branch and saw two or three women and a little girl in the process of making pottery. I really wanted to see how this was done and pointed in their direction. My new friend, oh my goodness, I had a Woodland friend, smiled and took my hand. She made a strange sound that I think maybe meant come. I followed her and in no time at all was sitting on the ground with them and they showed me how to dig the clay and mix it up with plant fiber. Then we pinched off some of the mixture and rolled it into little coils, placing one on top of the other. After that, one of the women gave me a smooth stone from the branch and showed me how to form and smooth the coil into the shape of a little bowl.

My new friend was just about to show me how to make designs on my bowl, when we heard a loud commotion near the skin huts. I looked up and saw Blue Sky Man coming toward me. He saw me and smiled. "There you are. I knew you would make friends."

"Is it time for us to go?" I asked, hoping that it wasn't.

"No, not yet," he answered. "There is more you need to see here. One of the children has taken ill and the shaman will attempt to heal him. You will be allowed to watch if you stay back and this will be one of the times you will need to be silent. Also, the shaman will perform the burial ceremony for an old man who is gone to be with the Great One in the sky. It was our good fortune that he died before we got here or, "Blue Sky Man paused.

"What?" I asked, already knowing the answered.

"We or you may have been blamed for his death. Come now, he replied.

"Wait, the child, what if he does not make it?" I asked softly.

"Then we will go, very quickly." Blue Sky Man proclaimed.

"I will be silent. Is there a shaman here?" I asked

"No, one was sent for from a nearby village. He has just arrived. Come with me. Remember, do not speak," he emphatically said.

I followed Blue Sky Man back to the group of Woodland people beginning to become more than a little frightened. The shaman, wearing a cloak of feathers, stood over the little boy. He held some sort of strange stone that opened on both ends in one hand and a pipe in the other. He first blew smoke in all four directions and repeated what seemed to be a chant over and over. Then, after taking something from his pouch, he placed it in one end of the stone object. Blue Sky Man told me later it was a medicine tube. After doing this two or three times, the child stirred and called out, I think for his mother. Blue Sky Man whispered, "the child is alright and so are we."

Soon after, the group, along with me and Blue Sky Man, begin to move toward a small clearing on the hillside. I noticed that two of the men were carrying a long stick with a big flat stone on the end, an early spade, and began digging. Then I noticed two other men carrying a bundle wrapped in deerskin. Oh dear, I thought, that's the deceased person. The bundle was placed in the grave, a stone axe and a string of stone beads were placed beside the bundle. Several men with spades covered the deerskin bundle with dirt and then others placed flat stones on top of the grave to prevent it from being disturbed.

During all of this, there had been silence but as soon as the burial was complete, the shaman began a loud chant and soon all the others joined in. The women were making a strange shrill sound, that I guess was keening. Whatever it was, it caused chill bumps to form on my arms. Then all was quiet again and the shaman blew smoke from his stone pipe in all directions and the Woodland people all returned back down the hill. Later Blue Sky Man told me, of course, most burials were in mounds, but one had not yet been constructed here, and they had placed the man instead in a grave.

Blue Sky Man told me to just wonder around and watch the people do their routine activities, that he needed to talk with some of his friends. "You will be fine. The women seem to have taken to you and they will be happy to teach you also. Might want to stay clear of the men though, I did notice that one or two of them had ugh," he laughed, "looked you over."

"You're kidding, right?" I asked, horrified.

"No, Missy, I am not. Just stay near the women, they will take care of you. I won't be too long, and then we will be on our way." He said as he walked toward three or four Woodland men.

I quickly spotted the women who had been making the clay bowls, and they motioned for me to join them. A large deer had been killed earlier, and they were in the process of removing the hide. I watched for a few minutes; afraid I was going to be sick. One of them handed me a sharp stone blade and showed how to hold it so that I would not cut myself. She then proceeded to show me how to remove the hide. So, I did, and it wasn't nearly as bad as I thought it would be. Here I am skinning a deer with Woodland women. Never in my wildest dreams could I have ever imagined this. Two women continued to work on the deer while the other two got up and motioned for me to follow. After washing our hands in the stream, one of them picked up baskets giving me one and we headed down the path, stopping in front of a big bush covered in berries. As we picked the women began talking to me as if I could understand. While I couldn't, I understood what they were trying to tell me. That the work of a Woodland woman was never done. Just as we were finishing with the berry picking and another project was about to start, I saw Blue Sky Man coming my way.

"So, Missy, they are showing you what it is like to be a Woodland woman." He laughed. "But it is just about time for us to move on." He said something to them in their language.

I was surprised to see a look of disappointment cover their face, like they were sorry to see me go. The first one, who I had contact with went inside her huti and came back with something in her hands.

"They are sorry to see you go," Blue Sky Man said. "Looks like you have made friends with the Woodland women," he paused. "She wants to give you something to remember them by. The only problem with that is that she will expect something from you in return."

I had nothing to give her except an inexpensive bead necklace that I had on, which I immediately took off. The Woodland woman walked to me and began talking in the Woodland tongue. She handed me a stone object, which Blue Sky Man said later was an effigy of a turtle and that I should feel very honored to have received it. Then I gave my necklace to her. She looked at it and her eyes began to sparkle with tears. Oh my, I thought. I had not expected this. She looked at the river and said, "Tal-la-poo-see."

Blue Sky Man took my hand, and we began to walk. "We're going forward into the future. We will go down the river to the towns of Talisi and Tuckabatchee," he smiled, "I think you are very familiar with these towns. The year is 1250 or so and we will be in the Mississippian time period."

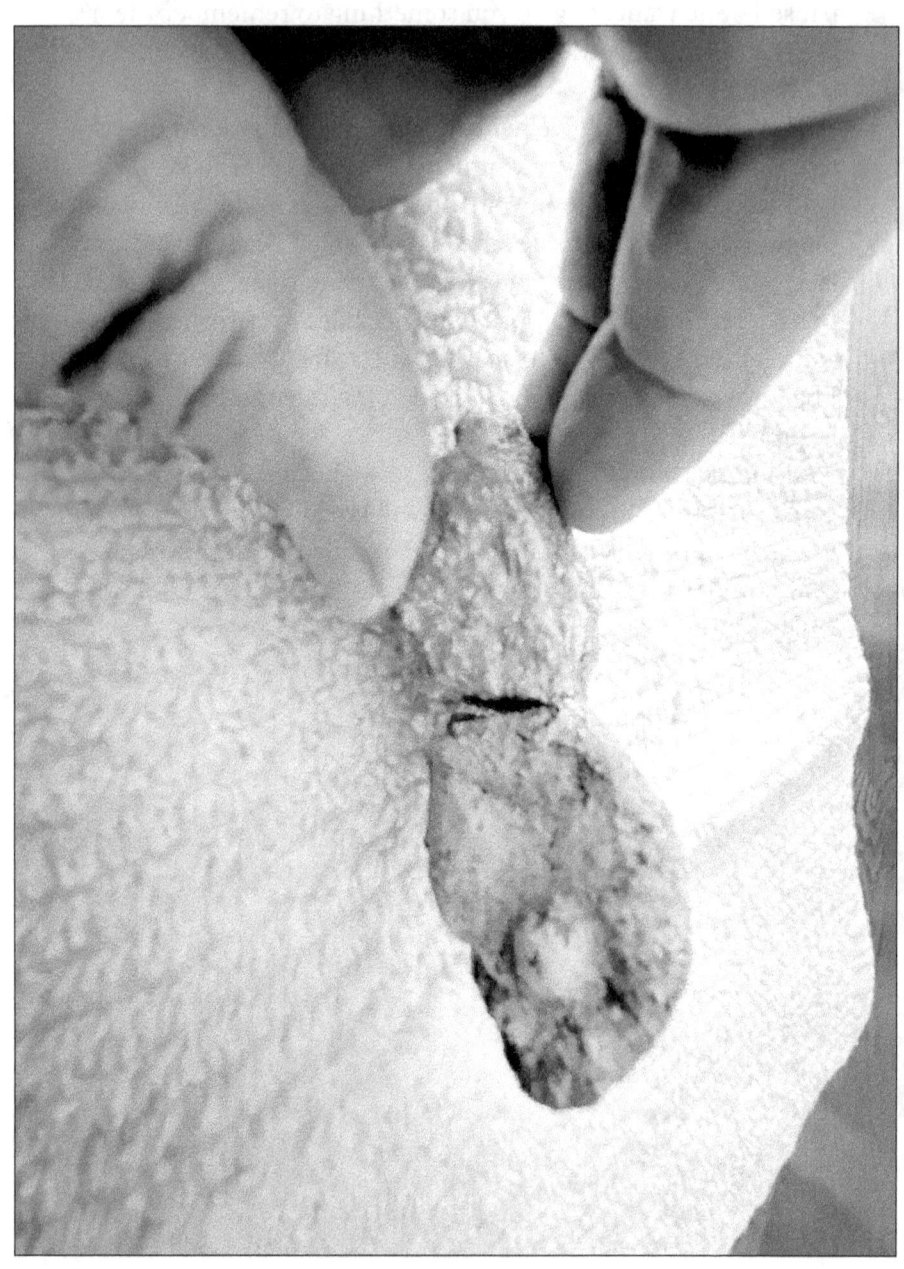

Woodland Period Stone Turtle was discovered at Pottery Spring which flows into the Tallapoosa River.

Chapter Nine
Stone Bridge

The cheerful song of the redbird singing and the mournful call of the morning dove welcomed me when I opened my eyes again. We stood beside a pretty little stream that seemed to have a yellowish tint. "Is this Yellow Water Creek?' I asked.

Blue Sky Man nodded, "Yes, very good."

"My husband and I have, while fishing on the river, came up this stream. My husband, will he be concerned about my absence?" I asked, "I seem to have been gone for a long while. I do not want him to worry about me. Is there any way to let him know that I am safe?"

"No, we cannot contact him, but we will not be gone for as long as you think. But remember, I told you that you can return at any point. Do you want to go now? You sure will miss a lot if you do." Blue Sky Man answered.

"No, I do not want to go back now. This is a wonderful experience. Unbelievable, but wonderful. One more question." I said, smiling.

"And that might be what Missy?" Blue Sky Man said, laughing at me. "Do you want to pinch me to see if I am real?"

"No, this is a serious question. Can I tell my husband about what I have seen and where I've been?"

Blue Sky Man became very serious and paused before he answered me. "That will be decided when you go back. You know folks will think that you are touched in the head if you go running around telling about this. We will see. Now, let me set the stage so you will know what is going on now."

I smiled at the old man in front of me and nodded. "Yes, please continue."

"Well, I know that you already know about the history of both towns, or you think you do. What I tell you and what you see may change some of that for you. Come, let us sit on this log and rest for a while before we get started." He pulled a big piece of tough looking meat from the skin bag at his side. "You still have your bag, don't you?"

"I do; it's under my shirt." I replied.

"Good, don't take it off. Here." Blue Sky Man said.

"What is it?" I asked.

"Deer jerky, silly. What did you think it was, a piece of pizza? You know I sort of like that pizza stuff. Think I might have me some when we return."

I knew that he was playing with me, but I really did not want any of this deer jerky. "No thanks, I am not really hungry." I answered.

"Better eat while you can. Never know how long it will be before you can eat again. Oh, by the way, you did good when we were with the Woodand people. Eating their food, I mean. That pretty much is what sealed their friendship with you." Blue Sky Man said, offering me his jerky again.

"Alright, give me some of your deer jerky." I said, thinking I hope it is better than it looks. I took a little bite and smiled. "Not too bad. Now tell me about what is ahead for me."

"Oh, you will find out that for yourself." Blue Sky Man said, licking his fingers. "As you know, both of the towns, Talisi and Tuckabatchee have been around for a long, long time. People have lived on the banks of the river for thousands of years. Had and old fellow tell me one time that he reckoned there was people here eight, maybe ten-thousand years ago. That's going all the way back to the Paleo and Archaic times. They came down following those big animals from a place called Siberia and finally made it all the way down here. They liked it here; it was warm most of the year and the forest and river provided them with plenty of food. Not sure when the people named the towns, you know that was not important to them all those years ago. Now you know, some of the modern folks," he paused and laughed, "the time you live in now, say which town was settled first and that Spanish explorer DeSoto, the one that was so cruel to Indian people came here. Well, some of the historians and fancy educated people have got into some pretty heated arguments about that. Some think, that without any doubt, he did and that he stayed on the banks of the river for several days."

"I, as well have done a lot of reading, trying to figure that out and have an opinion too." I added when Blue Sky Man paused.

"So, Missy, what do you think?" He asked me. "No wait, let me tell you first, then we can argue about it, but you know I will be right!"

I laughed at my new friend, this Blue Sky Man. I still had no idea how this was happening. Maybe it was a dream, but it sure did seem real if it was. "Alright," I said. "Tell me."

He took another bite of his deer jerky and slowly chewed with a far way look in his eyes, as if he was going even farther back in time than we already were, then he began to talk. "I had a good friend by the name of Woodward, part Indian himself, a Uchee I believe. I'm sure you have heard of him." He smiled at me again. "Shoot, you probably have the book of letters that he wrote about things. Now, he, of course did not live all that long ago, but he talked to the Indians who had the real truth passed down to them and this is what he told me.

'Blue Sky Man,' Thomas said, "this is the real truth that the people themselves told me. Tuckabatchee Town was settled a long, long time before the across the river town of Talisi. Now, you know that many towns had names that sounded almost the same and that also towns, over time, moved from place to place. And that's how folks got confused, I reckon. But Tuckabatchee was always on the west side of the Tallapoosa and was the first to be settled, no matter what others may say."

Blue Sky Man paused again. "And" he began, "tell you something else that some folks do not think of. Do you know where the mound is at Tuckabatchee?"

"Yes," I answered. "There was more than one in fact, but it was smaller and washed away when the river flooded. Plus, over the years, what was left of it was lost to cultivation." I answered, thinking that Blue Sky Man would think that I knew what I was talking about.

"That is true, actually there were several very close to Tuckabatchee and like you said, high water washed them down. So, Missy, how many were on the east side of the river?"

"I don't recall ever hearing or reading about any on the Talisi side, but I guess there could have been some at one time or the other," I said.

"That is true, but I don't know of any either. The point I want to make here is this. If Talisi was settled first, then why come there were no mounds? Mounds were built first by the Woodland people, you know that. And, as I told you and you saw for yourself, the Woodland people and others before them were right here. So, are you ready to move on? We will stay here, but the time period will be, oh about eleven-fifty or so. There is one more thing, I know you are familiar with the Mississippian period, right?" He asked and smiled as if he was going to tell me something that I didn't know. I nodded. "Historians and others asked the question, where did the Moundville people go? The town and the culture itself just seemed to vanish in a short period of time. You know that by then their main food source was corn, and they planted and harvested it in a great quantity. Also, they built mounds, many very large mounds. And finally, Moundville became a chieftain society, and the chief expected or may have demanded that his subjects plant and harvest as well as carry pot after hundreds of pots of soil to build these mounds. Since there was plenty of food, we know they did not starve and there was no evidence of any warfare or any disease that killed them, so, again where did the Moundville people go?" Blue Sky Man laughed. "Well, as time went by," he laughed again at the reference of time. "His subjects felt less and less responsible and inclined to pay homage to the chief. And you know what Missy? I think they just told him to plant his own corn and build his on mounds. And the people just left. And you know what else?" He asked, his bright blue eyes sparkling in the sunlight.

"What else? "I asked.

"Many of the Moundville people ended up way down here

on the Tallapoosa. So there, what do you think about that?" He asked.

"You sure?" I asked again.

"Missy, I was told that by some of their own people. So, I know for sure." He replied.

"Amazing!" I answered and was about to ask him another question when there was a sudden noise coming from the woods beside us.

Blue Sky Man signed for me to be silent, but it was too late. Four or five Indian warriors appeared from the path. Their scowling faces told me that we were not welcome here and that we were in danger.

I watched as Blue Sky Man stood and attempted to greet them in their language. They pushed him aside and grabbed me by the arm and roughly pulled me up from the log I had been sitting on. He looked as if he was going to strike me. Panic briefly covered Blue Sky Man's face, but he suddenly smiled when several more warriors entered the clearing. One of them seemed to recognize him. Blue Sky Man again repeated the words of greeting and this time the response was much more agreeable. The tall warrior smiled broadly and repeated the words of Blue Sky Man. He looked at the warrior who still held my arm and sternly spoke to him. I think he must have told him to turn me loose because he immediately dropped my arm. In might freight, I had not realized how much it hurt.

Blue Sky Man pointed at me and said, "My friend." In English and then a word I did not understand. Both men smiled and the tall Indian looked at me and said the word again. "Smile at him," Blue Sky Man said softly. "Everything is alright now. But that was a close call." He turned back to the warrior and the two of them talked more in the native tongue of the Indian.

Blue Sky Man turned to me and asked, "ready to go to the old town of Tuckabatchee? Don't think you will recognize it as a place you know. Remember now, the time period is around 1250. Things will have changed, but your dress is still alright. Don't know for sure how the women will take to you." He reached in his skin pouch and handed me a smaller pouch. If any of them give you a gift, you will need something to give them in return. There are several stone beads and small piece of copper or two inside."

"Blue Sky Man, wait. Will I be safe? Their women may harm me." I said, still rubbing my arm. "Please, stay close. At first anyway. And if this is Yellow Water Creek, aren't we on the wrong side of the river?"

"Of course," Blue Sky Man said in answer to my question and request. "We will cross the river on the stone bridge that was back up the river. You do know about the stone bridge, don't you?"

"I know, I even walked across it a time or two when the water was low." I answered, happy that I could impress Blue Sky Man.

I fell in line behind Blue Sky Man and the warriors, one of which brought up the rear and began walking up the path to Tuckabatchee Town. My goodness, I thought, this is unbelievable. I stopped short when we reached the stone bridge and was startled to see that it looked much like what I had crossed the river on before. The river was much lower, and I remembered that there were no dams to change the flow of the water then or now, wait which was it? I smiled. Guess I wasn't paying attention to where I placed my foot and suddenly, I felt myself slipping on the wet stone. Just as I was about to fall in the water, strong arms clasped me around my waist. I turned to thank the warrior and was surprised to see it was the same one who had so harshly pulled my arm before, and he still had the scowl on his brown face. Oh dear, I thought, I have made an enemy of this one. Our eyes locked and the scowl then turn to a smile. Then he began to laugh. He said a few words in his tongue and Blue Sky Man began to laugh too as he had turned to see what the commotion was all about.

"What did he say Blue Sky Man?" I asked, embarrassed.

"He said, woman with white skin had no skill to walk rocks." Blue Sky Man answered, still laughing.

I laughed with them, thinking they should see me try to walk a foot log. Soon after the close call, the town of Tuckabatchee came into view. Oh my!

Bridge Rocks stretch across the Tallapoosa River

Chapter Ten
Tuckabatchee Town

I had read much about the well known Tuckabatchee Town and even in this early time period, it was quite impressive. Many, many lodges made of waddle and dobb covered with what looked like several acres. Brown people were scurrying around, busy doing the assigned duties of the day. As we entered the village, after our arrival had been announced by the town dogs, some of which looked like they could have taken my leg off with one bite, all of them stopped their work and starred in confusion. I knew that none of them had ever seen a white woman, even my deer skin dress couldn't hide that I was white and different from them. The women talked among themselves, and one particularly mean looking one walked from the crowd and pulled my light brown hair. I jumped back with a cry of alarm and also pain. The women began to laugh. I looked at Blue Sky Man and silently employed him to help me. He then looked at the Indian man who seemed to be his friend and also the leader of the group of people. The man then looked at the women and spoke in a commanding voice. He continued talking and the woman, who had so rudely introduced herself to me by pulling my hair, then looked at me and smiled.

Much better I thought, and I smiled back at the group of women. Blue Sky Man and his friend talked on and then Blue Sky Man looked at me with his charming smile, "All is well now and again you go with the women, while I visit with my friends."

"Are you sure that I will be alright? They may all jump on me." I answered nervously.

"No, they will not harm you. Just be yourself. See you later," He laughed and walked off with his friend.

The women looked at me and started giggling, but I could tell they were not being malicious in any way. One of them motioned for me to follow them. So, away I went with the Tuckabatchee women, to do what, I did not know.

Immediately, I saw that there had been advancement since the last time period we had visited. I saw the difference in their houses, the dress and also that they had learned more about cultivation. I saw small stalks of corn as well as beans and squash being grown in the fields near the village.

One of the women, and I was surprised to see it was the same one who earlier had pulled my hair, motioned for me to follow her inside her house. Oh my, I thought, I'm seeing a real waddle and dobb house made from cane and clay. I stood in amazement as I looked at how the structure was meticulously put together. I knew it would be warm in the winter with a fire pit in the center and also that when it rained everyone would stay dry. The woman seemed to be looking for something and suddenly turned to me with a dress like she was wearing. It was similar to what I had been given earlier but was only one piece instead of a separate shirt and skirt. She handed me the dress and turned and went back outside. I quickly changed and placed the old clothing in my bag. I really hoped I could take all of this back with me. Then I remembered that Blue Sky Man had said a gift was reciprocal. So, I looked back in my bag for one of the clay beads that Blue Sky Man had given me. When the woman, oh I wish I knew her name and how to say it in her language, came back inside, I gave the bead to her. She smiled at me and said something that sounded like mudo. Did it mean thank you? She then touched her chest and said wa-na-new. I think she was indicating that was her name and pointed to me. I just said what Blue Sky Man called me. I repeated what she said and pointed to myself and said Missy. She said Mi-si and smiled and I knew I had a new friend.

One by one the women returned to their various duties and my new friend indicated that I should follow her. To my surprise she handed me a cane basket lined with skin and pointed to an area just outside the village. I saw several women and older children walking in the direction of a small pile of dirt. As we got closer, I realized that this was the beginning of a mound. "Oh, my goodness," I said out loud. Now I was going to help build a Mississippian mound. But where was the dirt to place on the mound coming from, I thought? The I saw several men and boys on the other side of the dirt digging in the ground. A borrow pit I thought. The women bending over were putting dirt in their baskets with a large spade. So, I did the same and filled my basket with the dark loamy soil. Then, as the women of the village watched, I slowly poured the soil on to the heap of dirt. Chill bumps instantly covered my arms. This was absolutely amazing! I guess this was going to be a burial mound and I wondered if like in the last time period I had visited, that if a high official of the village had passed away. We, me and the late Mississippian women continued for a while. And then I was beckoned away to participate in yet another work-related responsibility. Rubbing my back, I again followed my new friend, that I had now thought of as the hair-puller. We walked a good distance to the other side of the village where the community fields where located. I remembered when I saw the small mounds of dirt with stalks of corn and squash plants sprouting out of the center that this was the way the native people planted. Now, I realized it was our job to pull the weeds from around and in between the plants. We did this for awhile and although I could not understand what was being said, we seemed to form a comradery, laughing and talking to each other in a different language.

Then, one more time, I was motioned to follow Hair-puller, this time back to the village. She gave me a big, pretty pottery bowl and a pile of wild onions and other roots that looked like potatoes along with a stone knife and indicated for me to cut them up and place them in the bowl. When I had finished that, she took it from me and added chunks of meat. I had no idea what it was, and again it might have been best if I didn't. She then placed the mixture in a larger pottery bowl that was balanced on big rocks over the fire. She then indicated that we would eat this later.

I sure was getting tired, where in the world was Blue Sky Man. As I looked around, I noticed that the Indian men just seemed to be sitting around the fire, talking and smoking their pipes. I wanted to laugh but I realized that this was their way and that the women saw no wrong or humor in their behavior. I continued looking over the groups of men and search of Blue Sky Man. Ahh, there he is, I thought, sitting right in the middle of a group of warriors, obviously enjoying himself.

He saw me and waved but indicated that I should stay put. I knew that the women were not allowed among the men at this point. This was their thing. So, I turned back and was given yet another job to do. This time Hair-puller gave me two large pieces of deer hide and a bone awl along with sinue. I looked at her in confusion. She smiled and showed me how to sew the pieces together. Wasn't sure what I was making, but I think I did it right as Hair-puller nodded in approval.

Alright, now I was hungry and tired. When were we going to stop all this work and eat some of that food that smelled pretty good? Soon I saw Blue Sky Man walking toward me with his big smile.

"Have a good time?" He asked.

"Yes, I did," I answered. What about you?"

"Of course, I got to talk with my old friends," he laughed, "no pun in that. Soon as you women," he laughed again, "get us men some food ready and we eat, then we will be on our way. You know, I told my friend to tell his woman that we had traveled a long, long way and that you wanted to know how his people lived. So, she showed you, didn't she?" Blue Sky Man said, smiling. "I have watched you and you have done very well. I think you would have made a good Indian maiden."

Hair-puller tapped me on the shoulder and handed me several small pottery bowls and indicated that I should fill them with the stew mixture and give them to the men who had gathered around the fire. Then I filled one for Hair-puller and myself. "Good," I said as I dipped my wooden spoon into my bowl and tasted what I had helped to make.

Soon after Blue Sky Man told me to bid my newly made, temporary friends farewell, that it was now time to go. I was not surprised when Hair-puller pulled a string of shell beads from the pouch from her waist. I immediately pulled a large piece of shinny copper form my pouch and we exchanged our gifts to each other. She was obviously very proud of the copper. Then she smiled and mischievously reached up and pulled my hair.

Blue Sky Man took my hand, and we walked a short distance away from the Mississippian village of Tuckabatchee and we were gone.

Willow trees grow out of borrow pit where soil for a mound was gathered.

Chapter Eleven
Unfriendly Welcome

Moments later I opened my eyes to quite a different scene. Blue Sky Man told me that the date was now 1350 A.D. and we were still in Tuckabatchee. He reminded me he had earlier said some of the people of Moundville had migrated here to the banks of the Tallapoosa, bringing their culture with them. There were many, many more people and their houses stretched for as far as I could see. The houses were still pretty much the same except seemed a little sturdier. The clothing worn by the now Mississippian People, to my surprise had not really changed too much, still mainly deerskin. Neither of us said anything as we sat taking in the activities of Tuckabatchee Town, the soft coo of the dove and the cheerful song of the blue bird filling the air.

"Missy, we are at this time period just to see and observe how they lived. We will have no communication with them, in fact, they will not be aware of our presence," Blue Sky Man said suddenly.

"Why?" I asked, being a little disappointed. I had enjoyed interacting with the earlier people.

"We would not be welcome here at this time," he answered me. "And would possibly be in danger. Seems that some of these people have formed an attitude about new people coming to their land."

"So, how do we keep from being seen? Maybe, we should just leave now." I replied.

"Oh, they can't see us, and we will only stay for a short time. There are some things you should see." Blue Sky Man answered me not wanting me to be frightened.

"What do you mean they can't see us?" I asked confused.

"Well, Missy, it's like this. If I have the ability to take us thousands of years back in time, I can surely make us invisible. Now, don't ask any more questions. Just watch. This is a very informative part of our journey," He smiled. "Now come, we will get a little closer to the town so that you may see everything." He saw the fear in my face and continued, "I do not mean to frighten you. I just did not want to take any unnecessary chances. Everything will be fine, and you will enjoy this part of our journey. Come, now," Blue Sky Man said.

We moved a little closer where we could see a large area of the village and sat down on a big log. Blue Sky Man settled down and leaned back against a big pine tree and motioned for me to come sit by him. "Missy, I don't know if you realize it or not," he paused, smiling at me again, "but many of the customs and rituals that were practiced in the historical time period began here in the Mississippian period?"

"Which ones " I asked, sitting down beside him. Pretty sure that I already knew some of them.

"Well, let's just watch and see if you can figure them out," he answered. Look closely for any difference in the Woodland period and the Mississippian, then think about the future historical times."

I watched closely as the Mississippian people went about their daily routine. The first thing I noticed was that most of the men seemed to have tattoos all over their nearly naked bodies and the hair style was different. Instead of hanging loosely, many had some sort of top knot on the top of their head. I mentioned this to Blue Sky Man, and he acknowledged that this was true but not necessarily anything that made any historical difference.

"Blue Sky Man," I said. "If the Mississippian culture built big mounds and you said the people migrated down here from the Moundville area, why then are there no large mounds in this area?"

"Good question, Missy," he answered me. "Yes, the mounds here on the Tallapoosa are small compared to others in large Mississippian towns. Many, as we said earlier are from the Woodland period. My best guess would be that the Mississippian people may not have arrived here soon enough, and the big mound period was coming to an end. You are doing good, keep going. Look over there," Blue Sky Man said, pointing to a large group of men sitting around a fire. They were drinking a black drink from a gourd-like cup and passing it around. In a few minutes, everyone of them got up, going away from the fire and started violently throwing up.

"The black drink?" I asked excitedly to actually see the Indian men drinking the liquid and what the results were.

"That was an easy one," Blue Sky Man said laughing. "And I bet you even know what the stuff is made from and the reason to drink it, don't you?"

"I do. Remember, Blue Sky Man, I have been studying these people in one form or another since I was a child. The drink is made from the leaves of an *ilexous-vomatoria* plant. It was not a native plant but a coastal one and was probably brought here by the native people. They drink it to throw up and purify their bodies in preparation for a hunt or a battle," I laughed, "but I bet they like the way it made them feel, although I don't think the taste was very good."

"You are right about all of that. It did not taste good. Very bitter," Blue Sky Man said, laughing at me. " I know cause I had some. Made me sick as a dog, it did. Now, what else did you see?"

I watched intently for a few minutes and noticed that the pottery was much fancier than the Woodland period pottery, and very pretty, some of it made into effigies of animals. Sort of like what was given to me earlier but much more intricate. I told Blue Sky Man about this observation, and he agreed.

"One of the things that is not visible to the eye is the caste system that formed over the years and was at a much higher level. There was a hierarchy of sorts and was due to the great wealth that was obtained from the vast, vast fields of maze that was grown here and at other Mississippian sites. Like I told you earlier. This is probably one if not the main reason the Mississippian culture declined. Remember that over time the close connection between the people and the head man declined as well. They did not always do what they were told. Now what else," Blue Sky Man paused again. "Oh, yes, this is not the season for Boskita or the Green Corn Ceremony as it was called in historical times, but that ceremony also began here in the Mississippian period."

I nodded, remembering that I had read that somewhere along the way too.

"We're going to just sit here awhile and then we will be on our way. Since we can not interact with them, there is really no need to stay, other than just to watch." Blue Sky Man said. "Think I will just take me a quick nap, you know I'm getting to be an old man." He winked at me and continued, "Don't leave this spot and wake me up in a few minutes." With that he closed his eyes and quickly began to softly snore.

I continued watching the Mississippian village and realized what an amazing experience this was. Then, I heard a sound behind me and was startled to see two Mississippian men looking at me. Blue Sky Man said we couldn't be seen, but it was very obvious that they could see me. Oh no, I thought, this is trouble. Before I could wake Blue Sky Man, one of them grabbed me by the arm. He was speaking in his native tongue, and I could tell that he wasn't giving me a warm greeting. "Blue Sky Man", I yelled, but the old man was sleeping soundly and did not stir. I was dragged into the village where those close by stopped what they were doing and looked at me in hostile amazement. Fighting the urge to scream, I did not fight the Indians and tried to remain calm, yeah right. I figured this was probably going to be the end of the line for me. My husband would never know what had become of me. The women seemed to be more aggressive, and several had picked up rocks, that I knew would be thrown at me. Just as a rock left the Mississippian woman's hand and I felt pain shoot up my arm, I saw Blue Sky Man running toward me with the look of fear on his face. I knew they could not see him. He ran to me and grabbed my hand and then strangely enough I disappeared from their sight. If I had not been so frightened and my arm had not hurt so badly, the sight in front of me would have been hilarious. The Mississippian people were very superstitious, and they must have believed that I was some sort of a witch from the underworld. The women started screaming and running around in circles while the men notched their bows preparing to defend themselves from they knew not what.

"Missy, I am so sorry, I should have never allowed that to happen. It was a close call." Blue Sky Man apologized as the people in front of us stood in confusion and fear.

Rubbing my arm and trying not to break down in tears, I answered my friend, "Blue Sky Man, I thought they couldn't see me," then I smiled, "but they could."

"Not real sure either, but it won't happen again. Remember, I told you these people do not like newcomers, but I think they were more afraid of you than you were of them. You did good again, if you had fought them, things could have been worse. Now, ready to go?" He asked, taking my hand and we left the unfriendly Mississippian town.

Chapter Twelve
DeSoto

Before I opened my eyes, I heard the humming sound of cicadas and smelled the heavy scent of late summer. Then I saw the Tallapoosa, the flow slow and easy. I knew we were back on the east side, and we were near the town of Talisi.

I smiled at Blue Sky Man and knew that he was still upset about what had happened during the Mississippian time period. "It's alright Blue Sky Man. No harm was done. This big blue spot on my arm will fade in a day or two. So, I know we are near Talisi, and it must be September, I think, but what is the year?"

He smiled back at me before saying, "Missy, you are a brave one alright. You are definitely the right person to make this journey. The year is 1539 and it is September, and we are near Talisi."

"DeSoto?" I asked excitedly to learn the truth about the famous but sad expedition that had changed the lives of the native people.

"Right, again," Blue Sky Man answered me. We can interact with the people this time, but you need to use extreme care if you find yourself around the Spaniards. They are a bunch of scandalous men. In fact, I don't think I will allow you anywhere near them."

"I would like to see DeSoto," I laughed, "but I think from a distance will be just fine."

"Alright then, let's go to Talisi Town. But you won't see DeSoto there." Blue Sky Man replied, "but wait, let's do this first. If you want to see the disgusting man we will go, only briefly, to a place where he really was." He took my hand again and suddenly we were at a different place on a different river, a much bigger river, the Coosa.

Blue Sky Man pointed, and I could see up the path, which had turned into a vast highway filled with men, their horses and more pigs than I have ever seen at one time, pushing their way through the virgin forest. They were led by a group of Indians who seemed to fear for their lives. As I watched, one of them was punched with the tip of a bayonet, blood pouring down his back as he fell to the ground, only to be pulled back up by the Spaniards and them pushed forward again. The entourage of men that followed were the most horrifying that I had ever seen. Then, there he was, the infamous Hernando DeSoto. His entire body, as well as the others of the group were covered in armor. His beady black eyes shining in the bright sunlight and the dark beard covered the bottom half of this face. He looked more vicious than any of the Indians that I had seen thus far. What an evil-looking man, I thought to myself. I heard him bark orders to his army of men, telling them to strike down anyone who stood in their way. As the entourage entered the village, the screams of the people were blood chilling, and I heard him demand to be taken to the chief.

"Had enough?" Blue Sky Man asked me, a look of sorrow covering his face.

I nodded. "Please take me back to the Tallapoosa." Before I could finish, he had taken my hand, and we were back on the banks of the familiar river that I call home. Tears filled my eyes as I sat down on a big rock by the river and covered my face.

"Missy, there's nothing we can do about what has happened. You know now that DeSoto and his army did visit the town of Talisi, but it was on the Coosa River not the Tallapoosa. Now, there will be those who will argue that, but that's alright too. Everyone is entitled to their opinion."

Before we go to Talisi Town, let's talk more about that town, then we will go. Runners had been sent and word spread very quickly that a vast number of people, that were not Indians," he paused and laughed, "but I doubt very seriously that they called themselves Indians. They were known and called themselves by the name of their town, many of which I cannot pronounce. So, that does not matter, but anyway our people knew they were coming and that they had caused harm to others, stole food and taken some as hostages. Word was, they were looking for the shiny rock, but the people knew none of that was to be found here, not much anyway. You know Missy, them were some bad folks alright. Coming here to plunder the land, take the women and cut down any of the men who got in their way. But that really wasn't the worst of it. The disease and sickness they left behind, a disease that might near took out a whole race of people." Blue Sky Man stopped, and I could tell he was reliving a sorrowful time in his mind.

"But anyway, our people waited. Not knowing for sure if he, DeSoto, was coming here. Fortunately, as you know now, the terrain was too tough for all the horses and," he laughed, "hogs. Don't know why they brought all them hogs here. Guess they thought that was all they would have to eat. You know that we have had hogs here ever since. But DeSoto and the main bunch of 'em, I think, kinda split the difference and came down in between the Coosa and Tallapoosa and missed our Talisi. Oh, the Talisi people did have a run in or two with some of 'em that was sent to check out the countryside. Don't think it amounted to much, most likely them Spaniards got themselves shot up with lots of arrows, and some made it through the armor too. And our people here did take a fancy to the metal objects they took from them, maybe even the brass plates that were talked about so much by them fancy historians. Now, that might be so, but I'm not real sure where the plates came from. Maybe, from the Shawne people who came here long ago. Also, some of them tried to say that the big battle, the one called Mabila was actually fought here, but that weren't true either. That battle took place over on the Alabama River. Of course, there's lots of things that now a day folks just don't know nothing about any how." He paused again and looked at me, "think it's 'bout time we mosey on."

"What time period are we going to go?" I asked curiously about where we were going. I still did not understand how this was happening, but I sure was enjoying this trip very much. By now, I trusted this Blue Sky Man completely and I knew he would return me home safely.

"How about 1685 and we will stay right here on the Tallapoosa River. Which town do you prefer, Talisi or Tuckabatchee?" He asked, barely giving me time to take his hand before we were time traveling again.

Chapter Thirteen
The Trader

Before I could get my balance good, we were already standing on the Tuckabatchee side of the river. As before the sounds of nature were loud and clear. The song of the redbird was especially sweet. The changes were drastic. Most of the people were completely clothed, the women in their deerskin shirt and skirt allowing me to almost fit in. A few of the men were still clad in the breechcloth, must have been a reason for that I thought. Their houses were crude versions of the sturdier cabins they would have in the near future. The Tuckabatchee people seemed to be excited about something, and I asked Blue Sky Man what was going on.

"Well Missy, the people are about to meet the first trader to come to these parts. Runners from the upriver town of Okfuskee told them he was headed this way, and they were excited to see what he had to show them." Blue Sky Man answered me. "Think this will be fun and not nearly as sad as what we just witnessed. Come, let's blend in with the crowd and watch them. I think I can hear him coming now."

I could hear the jingle of the bells coming from up the path and then I saw him just as the Tuckabatchee people did. A big man, his face covered with a reddish beard, his long hair the same color. He seemed jolly as the dropped the big blanket from his shoulder and yelled out a big hello to the people standing in front of him. I watched as all the people stepped back and gasped as the blanket fell open and revealed the treasures unknown. What lay before them was the likes of nothing they had ever seen before. Oh my, there were bright blue beads and white beads and even red ones with a dark center that looked black, but when held up to the sunlight was really green. I knew that because my husband and I had been really excited to find one in the old fields where we had looked for treasures from the past. There were copper objects, like the bells the trader had on himself that jingled when he walked. Many cylinder-shaped things, the people had no idea what they were. The women really liked the looking glass, they had never seen themselves before except their reflection in the smooth surface of the river. And the men were overjoyed by the iron hatchet. Oh, the shrewd trader gave out a few of the items to the lucky ones standing closer to him. The others, with the excitement of children converged to the blanket. Blue Sky Man, at that point went and stood in between the trader and his wares and the Tuckabatchee people. He knew they did not understand the new trade concept and thought this strange man came to their town bearing gifts, which they intended to reciprocate with something, but not what the trader wanted.

Blue Sky Man spoke sharply to the red-headed trader, telling him that the people did not understand what his intentions were. He then turned to the mass of the Tuckabatchee telling them in their own language what was expected of them in order to receive the trinkets of the stranger. Slowly, the disappointed crowd broke up and returned to the activities of the day. Some of the men did venture back to the square ground with a few of the requested deer skins. Blue Sky Man looked at me and sadly smiled, "Missy, you have just witnessed the beginning, the beginning of a tie that would bind the native people to the trader and his trinkets, the metal axe and the hoe. These were just luxury items in the beginning then they became items of necessity. A necessity that would change the lives of these people for ever and would eventually lead to their destruction and," he paused, "their demise."

Blue Sky Man had told me that the next hundred years or so, the period between 1685 and 1785 were his favorite time period for the native people. This was the time he had said, was the most peaceful time for them. The items the trader had brought had indeed made their lives much easier. This was the time before the great influx of white people invaded their land and would eventually take it from them.

We stayed with the people, first on the Tuckabatchee side and then on the other side of the Tallapoosa in Talisi. I enjoyed being with the women and made friends with many of them. They were really good women who worked extremely hard all of the time. I laughed when I thought of what the women of my time would thing and do under the same circumstances. Blue Sky Man, of course spent his time with the men, sitting by the fire, smoking their new white clay pipes that they had obtained from the trader. He also disappeared with a strikingly pretty woman. He smiled at me as he walked by and I thought immediately of the song from my teenage years, Traveling Man by Rick Nelson, a song about a man who had a girlfriend in every town. That surely described my friend Blue Sky Man.

I already knew, even before my 'time travel' experience, that this was my favorite time period of the native people too. They were at peace with each other and lived a good, happy life for the most part. Oh, there were the occasional disagreements with other native groups, but this was quickly put to rest by their diplomatic way of settling things. Of course, when the white man came to their land, this all changed.

All too soon, Blue Sky Man came and sat down by me as I listened to a woman talk. I don't know what she was saying to me, but her voice seemed to have a musical flow and was mesmerizing.

"It's time for us to move on. I can see that you are enjoying yourself, but we must go now. There is still much for you to experience." He said something to the woman who had been talking to me. She rose and hugged me and reached into her pouch that hung at her waist, pulling out a perfectly shaped muscle shell bead. I in turn gave her a trade thimble that Blue Sky Man had given me if I needed to reciprocate with a gift. She hugged me again and said goodbye in her Muskogee language and watched as me and Blue Sky Man walked from the village and then we were gone.

Chapter Fourteen
Tuckabatchee

In a span of only minutes, I opened my eyes, and I could tell we were still on the Tallapoosa. I saw no one, but heard the chopping sound of an axe, many of them. I looked at Blue Sky Man silently asking him the time period, not knowing for sure if we should remain silent.

"It is 1780 and it is alright to speak," he answered me.

"What is that chopping sound? Is someone trying to cut down every tree in the forest?" I asked half joking.

"Sounds like it, don't it," Blue Sky Man answered smiling with his big grin. "But sadly, it is the white man and all of their families. They have come and have decided to build their cabins close to the Muskogee people. Oh, remember, they call themselves Creek now." Blue Sky Man informed me.

"This is a sad time now for the Creek people," I answered. "Will we go into the village or stay on the outside and watch?"

"We will do both," he replied. "But remember you must not say one word about the future and what lies ahead for them. By the way, some of them have mastered the English language or can understand it anyway. So again, be careful of what you say to the women. I do not think you will have any reason to talk to the men. You can tell them that I am your uncle, and we are just traveling through these parts. Got it Missy?" Blue Sky Man answered me a little sternly.

I shook my head that I did understand. "Blue Sky Man are we in any danger here?" I asked quietly.

He smiled again and said, "scared you, didn't I? No, but there is still so much I want you to see, and I don't want to have to leave before we are finished with our time traveling. If something you said put us in jeopardy, then we would need to go straight back. Now, let us go watch and listen for a while."

We walked a little closer to the loud sound of the axe and falling trees. An area large enough to plant a small garden had already been cleared. There was and old man and two others that looked considerably younger looking at the job they had done. Must be a father and his sons I thought. This was confirmed when one of the younger ones said, "Pa, ain't we done good enough for one day? I's real tired. Sure could use some vitals."

"Boy, we's will rest when I say so. Now get ya back side back to work," the older man said. "Ya know that we's got to have a cabin here a'fores we's can claim this here piece of land. Now, Sam, ya keep a look out fer any of them sneaking Indian heathens. If'n ya see one, just shoot him where he stands." The man said to a younger son that I had not noticed who stood at the edge of the clearing holding an old flint lock musket.

"Yes sir, I aim to kill one of 'em afore we's through," the boy answered.

I looked at Blue Sky Man and he shook his head. We silently walked away. When we had walked far enough not to be heard, we sat down under a big oak tree beside the river. Blue Sky Man sat silently and watched the easy flow of the Tallapoosa. I knew that sadness had overcome him, and he was trying to work through it. He suddenly said, "it's sad Missy, it's almost more than I can bear."

"I understand, Blue Sky Man," I said softly.

"I cannot do anything about it, and I cannot change what will happened in the future or the outcome." He continued. I saw him wipe a tear from his bright blue eyes and then he smiled. "Come, let us go into the village. I think you will enjoy talking with the women. At this time the Creek people still did not know what the future holds for them. They are still happy and content. I have a few friends that I would like to visit with too." He smiled at me again and I was happy to see that he had overcome the sadness he had felt a few minutes before.

"Would one of them just happened to be a pretty Creek woman?" I asked, returning his smile.

"Actually, there are two, happen to be sisters, they are. And I also want to talk to the powerful man by the name of McGilvery. I know that he is here at Tuckabatchee now. So, enjoy yourself Missy," he paused, "but remember, they do not need to know of the future. So, careful what you say. I will be back for you when it is time for us to move on."

We walked for a few minutes beside the river path and soon entered the village of Tuckabatchee. We were met by a large group of Creek men and women who seemed happy to see Blue Sky Man. He introduced me as a relative this time and told the women to take care of me and then walked off toward the square ground with the Tuckabatchee warriors.

What a delightful time I had with the women. A few of them actually knew a few words in English and most of them understood what I was saying. They all had many questions about where I was from and why I looked so different from them. One even shyly said that my eyes were like the eyes of Blue Sky Man. They were happy that I wanted to join in and help them with their work and that I already knew what to do. I helped them weed the corn and beans, skin a deer and then they were surprised when I knew when to add crushed shell to the clay to make the pottery hold together. Of course, they had no way of knowing that I had been taught these things from the grandmothers and even their grandmothers. After our work was done, I followed them to the river where we all jumped in and frolicked like children. Then it was time to make the deer stew and sofkee for the midday meal for the warriors. "All hungry," one said. "Want to eat."

What a wonderful life these people had, I thought. Free from the pressure and rush of my world. Then I remembered what the future would be, maybe not for them, but surely that of future generations of their people. I could stop the tears that filled my eyes. They all looked at me and one asked in English, "why blue eye women cry?"

"You are all so happy," I began. I wish you could be…"

Before I could finish my sentence, I felt a tap on my shoulder and Blue Sky Man shook his head. "Missy!"

I looked at him and immediately understood that I was about to make a mistake and do what he had told me not to do.

"I just mean, I wish the people I knew were as happy as you." Blue Sky Man smiled and walked away, both of the pretty sister friends at his side.

After the midday meal was eaten, the warriors all gathered back in the square ground to again smoke from their pipes, some still using the ones they had made while others used the new white man pipe the had obtained from the trader, and there were many of those white stemmed pipes now.

There seemed to be much talk and many words that needed to be said. I would like to have been able to listen in, but I knew that I was forbidden to do that. I enjoyed talking with the women anyway and the afternoon quickly passed.

All too soon, I saw Blue Sky Man coming my way and I knew it was time. The Creek women were all sad to see me go and told me to come back for a visit with them again. One told me that the wife of her brother had walked the path to the Great Spirit when a baby boy was born too soon, and that the child had also walked. He would need a new woman, and she thought since I knew the way of the Creek, that I would be good for him. I smiled at her, knowing she was paying me a compliment, but that I had a husband waiting for me when I return from my trip. My husband, I thought, I hope he's not worried about me. I always told him where I would be except for this time. He would surely think I was crazy when I told him that I had been gone for thousands of years. Again, I wondered how this could be.

Blue Sky Man took my hand, and I waved to my new friends. As we vanished from this site, Blue Sky Man said, "there's still something I want you to see before we move on." We walked on up the path and came to a very large open space filled with knee high corn. Right in the middle stood a large tree. "Do you know the significance of the tree?" He asked.

"I do," I smiled. "That's the Council Tree, the Council Oak. It is a beautiful tree. Are meetings and councils already being held here?" I asked excited.

"Yes, in fact this morning I met with Alexander McGilvery

and a few other right under the branches. Missy, you know the history of this tree and that many, many issues of importance for the Creek people will be argued about and will be settled here." Blue Sky Man answered.

"I do know, Blue Sky Man. Thank you for showing me the tree. I have seen many pictures of the original one, but never thought I would actually see it," I answered as I gazed at the Council Oak, wondering if I might witness a council meeting myself.

"The old tree will have its share of damage from violent storms in 1909 and 1920, and also a fire in 1922. The original tree still remained standing in 1929 when a dedication marker was placed here beside it." Blue Sky Man remarked and smiled. "Of course, my old buddy Thomas Woodward swears up and down that the original tree was cut down by a tenant farmer when he owned the property. Also, one of them modern day archaeologist says that the tree probably dated back to 1836, but probably wasn't the tree we were looking at now. According to some, the location may not be exact either," he paused. "So, Missy, like many things in history the real truth sometimes gets lost in time or confused or even just plan lied about."

This time I smiled at my friend, "but you know, don't you Blue Sky Man?"

"Course I do. I sat underneath these branches many ah time listening to important chiefs and leaders make their talks, but I am going to let you decide for yourself about the Council Oak. But you know what, it really does not matter if there was just one tree or many, what matters is what happened underneath the branches of the tree and how the lives of the Creek people were changed," Blue Sky Man reflected.

Large tree in a distance was planted in the 1990s at the site of the original Council Oak at Tuckabatchee.

Chapter Fifteen
White Folks by the Thousands

I watched the Council Tree fade away as we again moved on through time. How in the world was this happening I wondered as I opened my eyes. I knew we were still on the banks of the Tallapoosa and that we had not traveled far. "The date," I asked?

"1805 Missy," Blue Sky man answered as he looked around like he was making sure we were not being seen. "I am going to do some talking before I show you anything else. We are now entering into one of the saddest and most turbulent time period the Creek people experienced. I know you have read and studied about this extensively, but now you will be able to actually feel their pain. Come, let us again sit by the river for a while." He reached into his pouch and pulled out two pieces of bread made from corn by the Tuckabatchee women and handed one to me. "Ya know, this bread ain't half bad, is it? A fellow could get use to this. Think maybe when we finish our traveling, I'll be heading back to the time before all the trouble and sadness started for the people, when their life was good. Think I might just stay with them for a spell, a long spell."

I could tell that my friend was again slipping back into that sad place in his mind. I realized that he had seen it all, the good and the bad times. He had seen the horrors that the Creek and the other native people had lived through. I understood his sorrow. I put my hand on his and smiled, "sounds like it is a good idea to me, but let's finish our journey."

He laughed, "Yes let's do that. Think you, Missy. Should have known you would understand. Now, back to what I was gonna tell you, "He leaned back against a big pine tree and begin to talk. "They came, oh, a few at first. Then they came from Carolina and Georgie by the hundreds, maybe even the thousands. So many came in fact, a road had to be constructed for them to travel over. You know all about that road they call the Federal Road. It was a fine road that started up on the east coast coming through Milledgeville, Georgia and went all the way down to Mobile, coming might near the Creek towns of Talisi and Tuckabatchee, it did. Made it easy to get across the little creeks and low land swamps that were filled with alligators and big ole cotton mouth moccasins." Blue Sky Man pause and laughed. "You know Missy, many of them fine folks had some encounters with some of them varmints, a few of 'em even got bit by a snake or got their leg torn off by a gator. The Creek men who stood back behind them big ole trees would help the women and children if they got in trouble, but they kinda let nature take its course with the men."

"Blue Sky," I interrupted, "remember a while ago when you told me about the man and his sons clearing the land and one of the boys said he would kill him and injun or two?" My friend nodded, "Well, did he kill anybody?"

Blue Sky Man smiled again. I was becoming so accustomed to that smile and knew when it was coming. "Yes, someone got themselves killed alright, but it was not any injun. The old man and the big mouth son both took arrows near their hearts and that was the last of 'em. This kinda thing happened often. The white folks were so busy cutting down trees that they did not take time to watch out for the Creeks. This activity continued for the next few years. More and more white folks came, closer and closer to the Creeks. Course, the Creeks didn't like it one bit. Their hunting land was being robbed by the whites that took the deer and other sources of food that should have been for the Creeks. The white folks brought their cows and their mules, of course. So, the Creeks thought if whites stole from them then they should retaliate and steal livestock from the white. Many young braves got their back side busted with shot and a few of them did not make it back to their villages at all. Missy, you know things got seriously out of hand. The government men came with their treaty talks and promises that turned out to be just plain lies. Then things got really bad when the Creeks started fussing between themselves and the group that called themselves Red Sticks was formed. I know you know all about them and if I guess right, you probably would have been one on them too!" He laughed.

"Yep, you got that right," I laughed too. "I sure would have been."

"Me too, I think that's enough talk for now. Ready to go listen in on a council meeting underneath the branches of the Council Oak?" I nodded. "Then let's go!"

Just before Blue Sky and me arrived at Tuckabatchee Town, he handed me a shirt and britches that looked like some of the Creek men were wearing now. "Put this on, tuck your hair underneath this bandana, keep your head low and do not say a word. Think we can pass you off as an older Creek boy. I will say you are my kin if anyone ask. Ready? "

I nodded and followed Blue Sky Man to council. Oh, my goodness.

Chapter Sixteen
Tecumseh

We walked right up to the tree and Blue-Sky Man motioned for me to sit down behind the Creek men. I looked at him as if he was crazy. He smiled and whispered that everything would be alright. I watched as several of them came over to greet Blue Sky Man. I then realized he was known by them and was considered a friend. I still did not understand how I could pass off as being a Creek boy, but so far no one paid me any attention at all.

Just as the sun moved to the mid-point in the sky, a large man with spots all over his face and arms walked up to the crowd of Creek men. Big Warrior I thought. I am looking at Chief Big Warrior. Oh, my goodness. The Creek men, who had been talking among themselves all became silent and waited for the big man to speak. It was obvious that he had their respect.

"My brothers, I have called you here on this day to speak of the great number of white men and their women who have come to the land of the Creek people. They move closer and closer to our villages and expect us to," he paused and in a louder voice said, "get out of their way and then take what is ours. We cannot and will not allow this to happen. We have been told by the white man who calls himself Hawkins who today has traveled to the Chattahoochee, that we need to learn from the white man and become more like them. He said that would be better for us."

The Creek men all in unison jumped up and began to yell and shout. I had not heard such and became a little nervous. Blue Sky Man looked at me and signed that everything was still alright. We listened to several others talk and the excitement continued to escalate. I noticed that there were a few of them that did not seem to agree and realized that I was seeing the rife that would form between the Creek people and also the Red Stick faction become stronger.

Blue Sky Man thought it best that after the talks were over

and he spoke briefly with Big Warrior, that we should go forward with our journey. I watched, this time as the scene before me faded away and was soon replaced by yet another. We were still on the Tallapoosa, and I could see the Council Tree, her limbs swaying in the soft breeze. The warm air smelled of late summer. In the stillness of the day, I heard the unmistakable roar of the upriver falls and the closer sound of the rapids as the water rushed over the large granite stones in the middle of the Tallapoosa. I looked at Blue Sky and again received his smile that promised that exciting events from the past would soon be revealed to me.

"Enjoying this journey, are you Missy?" He asked. "Absolutely!" I replied. "Can't wait to see what happens next," this time I smiled at him, "would a visit from a warrior from the north be upcoming?"

"You are right Missy, he answered. "It is September 1811 and soon Tuckabatchee will be filled with not only the warriors of the Creek Nation, but the Cherokee, Choctaw, as well as others, and of course Tecumseh himself. You'll be able to see for yourself what actually happened. For now, let's go into the village, maybe get some sofkee and bread," He paused. "So, how do you like the way sofkee taste," Blue Sky Man asked, smiling.

"Not bad," I replied. "Different, but not bad. I like it with honey or berries better than plain."

"Me too," Blue Sky Man said as we began to walk. "I will drop you off with a friend of mine and then go talk with some of the warriors before we make our way back to the Council Tree. As you know, many, many warriors will be attending this council."

"Oh, by the way Blue Sky Man, will this friend of yours just happened to be a pretty Creek woman?" I asked mischievously.

"Why Missy," he laughed, "you know for sure that I will see her later."

I enjoyed my time with the friend of Blue Sky Man. I had taken my bandana off and let my hair hang free. I told her I was dressed as a man for more comfortable travel and that we had come a long way in a short period of time. If she only knew I thought. Blue Sky Man had quickly ate his bowl of sofkee and bread and told the Creek woman, and she was very pretty, that he would see her later.

She understood English and could speak it some as well. She told me in her broken English that she feared for her people and that she could see the change that had happened since the white man with his family had come. She said she feared war would come too and that many of her people would suffer and die. I couldn't tell her that what she feared would indeed come true. I hugged her when Blue Sky Man came and said it was time for us to go to the Council Tree.

I tucked my hair underneath the bandana again and assumed the identity of a young Creek man. I was amazed at the number of Native American people who had amassed under the big oak tree. They all stood in silent anticipation as word had been announced that Tecumseh was near the village.

The eyes of thousands of Indians were focused on the man as Tecumseh entered the square ground of Tuckabatchee. Just as I had read about him, he was indeed one of the most impressive men that I had ever seen. He and the group of eight or ten native men of different tribes that accompanied him were dressed in only breech clothes. Their menacing faces were painted black, the feather of an eagle attached to the top knot of hair on their heads and ornaments adorned their arms and necks. I along with all the other on lookers stood mesmerized as they walked around the square ground. I noticed that Tecumseh did have a distinct limp. He stopped in front of Chief Big Warrior, both glaring at each other in contempt. I knew that Big Warrior did not share the same opinions as the Shawnee Warrior and that by now Tecumseh was aware of that. Both, being men of integrity, the moment soon passed, and greetings were given and in a show of good will, tobacco was given to Big Warrior.

Blue Sky Man and me were the only ones in attendance that knew what would happen next. To the disappointment of all, Tecumseh declared in a loud voice that "the sun was too low in the sky." He would not give his talk on this day.

Blue Sky Man nudged me and indicated that we would go. I was disappointed. I really wanted to hear at least some of the Shawnee warrior's speech. "No, we are not leaving, we are just going to fast forward for a few days." He took my hand and before I could close my eyes, we were right back where we had just left. Amazing, I thought. There were even more warriors and chiefs waiting to hear the talk of Tecumseh than before.

September 19, 1811...

The sun was hot on my face, and I could again hear the distinct sound of the upriver falls and the closer call of the redbird singing his late summer song. I heard the unmistakable cry of a redtail hawk high in the afternoon sky. Then, total silence as the Shawnee warrior followed by his entourage entered the square ground. The same ritual of blowing smoke from a ceremonial pipe and in all four directions was done as on the first day of his arrival. Then, the impressive warrior stepped forward.

"My brothers," Tecumseh began. "My brothers, I have come here to the home of my mother to talk to you about the future of our people."

Some two hours later after sentiments of both anger and sorrow, Tecumseh ended his talk with a plea for all to join with him. Most of the warriors, both Creek and the others cheered and waved their red sticks high in the air in agreement with what had been said. Then there were some, including Big Warrior, who did not agree, they walked away in silence.

Tecumseh would stay in the town of Tuckabatchee for several more days. While there he promised that a light would fill the night sky, and it did, to the horror of all who witnessed the sight. I smiled when I saw the sight, which I knew was a comet and had been predicted by an astronomer friend of Tecumseh. Just before leaving he confronted Big Warrior telling him he did not believe the words that had been said, but that he would believe. Tecumseh stated in a solemn voice that when he returned to his Ohio home, he would stomp his foot and the houses of Tuckabatchee would fall to the ground. This happened too! I could not figure this out myself. Yes, there was an earthquake, the New Madrid Earthquake that flattened house from Missouri all the way to Alabama. But how did Tecumseh know this would happen? Blue Sky Man told me that by now I should believe in supernatural powers. Maybe he was right!

Chapter Seventeen
William Weatherford

I had heard the powerful Tecumseh speak and had witnessed the major split of the Creek Nation and saw the spirit of the Red Stick Warriors. I knew what the future held for these people but could do nothing. The next two decades would indeed be a time of much sorrow for not only the Creek, but for all of the Native people of this land. Blue Sky Man had said the fighting and pain would probably be more than I could bear, but he wanted me to see the end, which we would but first there were some men he wanted me to meet.

"Ready?" He asked.

"Yes, where are we going now?" I asked in return.

"Oh, over on the Coosa River and we will move forward a little bit. Know about Hickory Ground, right? How would you like to have supper with Mr. William Weatherford?"

"Are you serious?" I answered excitedly.

"Yes, Missy, here we go," he took my hand, and we were soon standing on the banks of the Coosa River at Hickory Ground. Like Tuckabatchee and other large Creek towns, this was a busy town bustling with activity. Blue Sky Man told me that here too, there was division and discontent. Some liked the new ways of the white man while others admittedly refused to accept it. Then there was the problem of the land … the white man wanted it.

While many had refused the way of the white people who had infiltrated their land, it was obvious that this man here did not seem to mind their ways at all. I saw many of the cabins of the white family and fewer of the crude homes of days gone by and was not surprised when we stopped in front of a nice cabin with pretty flowers planted in the yard.

"Hello, inside," Blue Sky Man yelled.

I was caught off guard and did not realize who lived in the house. A man who looked to be in his mid-forties with dark penetrating eyes and ruddy completion came to the door. Not totally white, has some Creek blood I thought. I was totally surprised when Blue Sky Man greeted the man.

"Hello Bill," Blue Sky Man said, laughing.

"Blue Sky Man," William Weatherford exclaimed as the two clasped arms in the Creek way of greeting. "It is so good to see you again. Come on in."

"Bill, I would like for you to meet a friend of mine. I just call her Missy," Blue Sky Man said happily.

"Hello, Missy," Bill Weatherford said. "It is nice to meet you. Any friend of Blue Sky Man is a friend of mine too."

I stood with my mouth open, "Hello sir, I stammered. "I have heard so much about you."

"From me of course," Blue Sky Man said, giving me a reproachful look.

"Yes sir, and it was all good," I said, regaining my composure.

I was shocked when we walked inside. The furnishings were that of an affluent white man with the exception of a Creek basket and a couple of pottery jars on the mantel above the fireplace. A very pretty woman who was obviously a me`tis, was sitting by the window mending a broadcloth shirt.

"This is my friend Blue Sky Man," Bill Weatherford said,

"You do remember him, and Missy, a friend of his. This my wife Polly."

"Hello Blue Sky Man and hello mam," Polly said politely in perfect English.

The two men exchanged small talk for a few minutes, then Blue Sky Man in a serious tone quietly said, "Bill, I need to talk with you in private. I have some news regarding the current situation in the Creek Nation that you should know."

"Certainly, Blue Sky Man, "Bill Weatherford replied. "Tell you what, you and I will go outside and sit by the river to talk." He looked over at his wife and said, "Polly, honey, I think a nice supper for our guest would be in order. Maybe you and Missy here could fix us something while we talk. How 'bout beef steak and some those fresh potatoes and gravy. How does that sound to you Blue Sky Man?"

"Perfect," Blue Sky Man answered seemingly always ready to eat.

The men went outside, and I followed Polly across and open hallway into a room with a big fireplace and large wooden table. A dog trot of course, dog trots would be in use by this period. What was the date, between 1812 and 1814 I thought. I knew the big battle at the Horseshoe had not yet occurred. Must be around the time of Burnt Corn.

"This is a very nice kitchen Miss Polly," I said hoping to form a good relationship with this pretty me'tis woman.

"Kit-chen," she answered me, puzzled.

Oh, my goodness, I thought. How do I correct this? "I, mean," seeing a little yellow kitten scamper out the door, I quickly said, "what a pretty kitten and this is a really nice," I paused, "nice cook room."

Polly nodded, "oh, yes, it is. Thank you. Do you have one like this where you live?"

"Not nearly as big as this," I answered, relieved. "But I would love to have one just like this." And I really would, I thought.

"Where do you live, Missy?" Polly asked, as she cooked the beef steak in a big pan that had hung over the fire.

"Over on the Tallapoosa," I answered happily. She smiled and we continued to talk about the little things that women of any time period shared.

Soon, we had supper ready, and I had helped Polly set the table with beautiful Blue Willow China. Amazing I thought just as we finished, Blue Sky Man and Bill Weatherford, Bill Weatherford Oh my I thought, came back inside. Both men looked serious but that quickly changed to big smiles as they smelled the tantalizing beef steak.

We all enjoyed our meal together and Polly and I became fast friends. I was so impressed with Mr. William Weatherford. He was a kind, good hearted man who loved his people, not a Red Stick devil as some would proclaim him to be. I was a little sad when Blue Sky Man said it was time for us to move on. We said our goodbyes to the Weatherford's and walked up the path out of their site forever, for me, and then we were gone.

Chapter Eighteen
Mims

Back on the Tallapoosa again, Blue Sky Man and me found ourselves sitting on the bank of the river. I realized that he relished watching the flow of water, at times swift and fast, then slow and tranquil. Blue Sky Man seemed almost mesmerized as the water flowed by us and I was hesitant to break the silence. Then he began to talk, "you know Missy, this is a special, beautiful river. It is almost like the flow of time. The water you see one minute is not what you see the next. Its already gone, just like time."

I nodded, kinda understanding what he was saying. He smiled sadly and seemed to be back to his old self. What a strange man he is I thought to myself, but then again, he had a right to be. I was sure that he was definitely one of a kind. Most people do not go wondering back and forth through time.

"Missy," he said cheerfully, "I have one more person for you to meet and it just so happens that he is here now.

I noticed that we were on the east side of the river, so that meant that we were in Talisi Town. "Would that be Peter McQueen?" I asked again, excited to meet the most ferocious Red Stick of them all. I also knew that Talisi was a Red Stick town.

"Yes mam, it is," Blue Sky Man answered me. "I want to warn you that he is not quite as, ah, a gentleman as William Weatherford was, but he will treat you kindly. Ready?" he asked. I shook my head. "Then come, let's go."

I could see that the homes of the Talisi residents were more like little huts and not the nicer dogtrot cabins at Hickory Ground. But of course, I only saw the home of Mr. Weatherford. As we walked up the slight hill to Talisi, I heard loud voices of men quarreling, one was very distinct and louder. I guessed correctly that it was Peter McQueen.

Blue Sky Man held up his arm for me to stop. "Think maybe we'll wait until things settle down a bit before we continue."

"We will leave before brother sun shows his face on the

new day," the loud voice announced with finality. The crowd of Creek warriors became silent in obvious consent to their leader. "Now let us have our sofkee and meat before we go to the square ground to make our plans for our trip to Pensacola."

"Now, we can go," Blue Sky Man said.

"Am I a Creek boy again?' I asked, hoping that I could be myself.

"No, it will be alright for you to be a woman. I will introduce you as my friend this time. Don't need to talk too much, Peter would not like a woman who talks a lot."

Peter McQueen looked up and saw us coming. "Ah, Blue Sky Man," the Red Stick leader announced. The two men clasped arms. "Blue Sky Man, it is so good to see you." He looked at me and asked, "who do you have here?"

"This is my little friend. I just call her Missy. She and I have just been ah, doing some traveling around."

The Red Stick leader, who looked more Creek than William Weatherford, gracefully bowed his head to me. "Good to meet you mam, may I ask you to allow me and your friend here to have a private talk. We have important words to say. You may go and visit with the women," he pointed to a group of Talisi women, preparing food for the warriors.

"It is very nice to meet you Mr. McQueen," I answered, more than just a little intimidated by the forceful man. "I will be happy to help the women," I looked at Blue Sky Man and smiled reassuring him that I would be alright and began walking toward the women.

They, of course were a little startled when I walked up, but since most of them understood and could speak a little English, we were soon chatting like old friends. My goodness, I thought, how much the Creek women were like the women of my time.

It wasn't too long before I saw Blue Sky Man walking toward me and he said it was about time for us to go. The Creek women all seemed to know him and both of us were offered sofkee before we left Talisi Town and they also wanted to visit with him. What a Casanova I thought.

When we had finished our sofkee and Blue Sky Man visited with the women, we walked away from Talisi Town. When we neared the end of the village, just at the border of a large stand of oak trees, I stopped and looked back at the village. Blue Sky Man looked at me and asked if something was wrong? "No, I answered almost in tears. "Remember, I have been here in my modern time period. My husband and I have done what we are doing now. Looking at the village, in our case, the old village site. I knew, just as I know now, that one day, very soon, it will no longer be here."

Blue Sky Man looked at me understanding completely what I was talking about. "Oh Missy, you are so right. You are a very perceptive person. Before we go, let's sit by the river and talk for a spell."

We found a small clearing by the river path and sat down and Blue Sky Man began to talk. "Missy, what did you think of Peter?" He asked.

"Didn't get much of a chance but I think he comes across as a tough guy when he is really not so tough at all. He is just a man, in that position, the one in charge," I answered, wishing that I could have talked with him a little bit more.

"There you go again, you got that one right too," Blue Sky Man answered patting my hand. "Peter fears for his Creek people. He is part white himself and he knows the strength and numbers of the white man. You know the trip to Pensacola was to obtain guns and ammunition from the Spanish. You also know that he received very little and most of what he received was taken from him at Burnt Corn. Of course, you know that retaliation would come and what would happen next."

"Fort Mims," I said softly.

"Yes, do you want to go there?" Blue Sky Man asked. "It will be very painful to see, a scene you will never be able to forget."

I took a deep breath and replied to Blue Sky Man. "I think I would like to go there but only for a very brief time. I want to feel the sorrow of the people, both the white and the red. I want to know what they endured on that sad day."

"Alright," Blue Sky Man answered me. "The date is August 30th, 1813. You know that over 250 whites, me`tis, friendly Creeks and others along with about that many soldiers had gathered at the home of Samuel Mims. I want you to pay close attention to details so that you will know the truth. Missy, if at any point you feel we should leave, please just tell me."

I nodded, a big lump forming in my stomach. What was I getting into? But it was too late now to change my mind. Blue Sky Man had my hand, and we were gone. I could feel the warm sunshine on my head and the heavy smell the of the Alabama River. I heard the sounds of children at play and the sweet sound of a violin and the voices of many people laughing and talking. We were positioned well away from the now fortified homes, but still close enough to see inside. I remembered what Blue Sky Man had said about details, and I saw the gate. I saw sand piled up high and I knew the gate would not close. I saw a soldier, General Beasley, I thought, his shirt unbuttoned and giving orders to be left alone. There were no Indians anywhere around he said in a slurred voice. I caught my breath when I saw movement in the bushes. I saw the Creek Warriors, many of them, their menacing faces streaked red and black. They stealthy walked through the bushes and trees, completely unnoticed by the unsuspecting people inside. The farm had been completely stockaded, there was no place for them to go.

I looked up, the sun was directly overhead and suddenly the screams of hundreds of what sounded like devils filled the air. Someone attempted to close the gate, then realized, because of the piled-up sand, it would not close. I saw a man, I remembered was a me`tis by the name of Bailey. He fought bravely, stopping to help some women and children to flea to safety. Minutes later, I saw him fall to the ground, an arrow protruding from his chest. In a matter of seconds, the opening was filled with Creek Warriors, William Weatherford in the lead. I could not believe the difference in his appearance. The people ran for their lives to one of the various buildings inside the stockade and a plan of defense was formed. I saw a child attempting to run to his mama and was knocked to the ground. I placed my hand over my mouth trying not to scream. To my amazement one of the leaders bent down and pulled the child from the path of the oncoming warriors. It was William Weatherford.

Blue Sky Man looked at me and quietly asked if I was ready to go? I did not want to but realized that I could not deal with the horrors of death that was soon to happen. "Yes," I whispered. Just before Blue Sky Man took my hand, I recognized the deep voice of William Weatherford yell, "spare the women and the children." Then we were gone, and I would forever remember what I had seen.

Chapter Nineteen
The Horseshoe

We stood on the bank of a swift narrow river, but I did not know which one. "Where are we?" I asked Blue Sky Man.

"Oh, we are on the Tallapoosa about thirty-five or forty miles up from Talisi." Blue Sky Man answered.

"We are at the Horseshoe then?" I said softly.

"Yes, we are," Blue Sky Man answered. "But we are not quite at the time yet of the battle. Let's talk a little about Fort Mims and what happened afterwards."

"I know you heard Bill Weatherford tell his warriors to spare the women and children and you saw him save the child that fell to the ground in the path of the rushing warriors. He tried desperately to prevent the carnage that happened at Mims. The first attack by the Red Sticks was bad enough, but it was in the second that so many of those poor people perished. The white folks and me`tis did what was only natural and tried to defend themselves. That is when things got out of control and Bill could not stop them." Blue Sky Man said softly.

"Blue Sky Man, how many people were killed?" I asked.

"Well, some say over five-hundred, others say just over three. I think it was closer to three-hundred, fifty or so. I do know that only about thirty-five or forty survived. But if you count all the Red Sticks, and there was a lot of them that died too, it could certainly have been 500 or more." Blue Sky Man replied.

"Blue Sky Man, where you there? Did you see?" I paused, wiping the tears from my eyes. Did you watch it happen?"

Blue Sky Man nodded his head. "Yes, Missy I did. I wasn't involved in the killing, but I saw it all." We sat in silence, Blue Sky Man with his vivid memories and me, having seen enough to feel the sorrow.

"I just wanted you to know Missy, that Bill Weatherford, for the rest of his life, regretted what happened on that day. He was torn between his white blood and his red. He never lived it down although he did again become a prominent citizen in the Lower Alabama area of Tensaw.

Did you know that Fort Mims and the battle of Holy Ground were the only battles that Bill actually took part in? But the whites still considered him a Red Stick heathen." Blue Sky Man continued talking and I did not interrupt. "Missy, the Red Sticks were only trying to save their homes and the land of their grandfathers, but so, so many were lost. In the battles of Autossi, Calebee, Talladega and all the others, hundreds were lost. In the end the native people lost their land anyway." He paused again, shadows of pain covering his face. "We won't go to these battles, but I want you to see some of the big one, the Battle of the Horseshoe."

He took my hand for a brief moment then we were on a slight rise on the opposite side of the river. I saw the makeshift village of Tohopeka filled with the women and children from Okfuskee, New Yonka, Hillabee, Fish Pond and Emuckfa.

"Today is Sunday, the 27th day of March 1814," Blue Sky Man informed. "Menawa has his warriors ready, the barricade that stretched from bank to bank in the curve of the Tallapoosa that forms the horseshoe has been constructed. Scouts say that Sharp Knife Andrew Jackson is almost here." Blue Sky looked up at the sun in the brilliant blue sky. "It will soon be ten o'clock."

I knew that was the time the battle would begin. I noticed some of the warriors were saying farewell to their wives and children as if they knew what the outcome would be. I saw on particular family, an impressive-looking warrior, a beautiful woman and two children, a boy and a girl about eight or so. They must have been twins, I thought. Their farewell seemed to be more poignant and intimate than the others. "Blue Sky Man," I said. That family seems to be different. Who are they?"

He smiled at me. "Why Missy, I think you know them. That is Soaring Eagle and his wife Little Flower."

"You are kidding me, right?" I exclaimed, surprised.

"No, that is who they are. You know their story," Blue Sky Man answered, smiling.

I heard the sharp rap of a drum and Menawa motioned for his warriors. "Come," he said. "The time is now."

I watched as the Creek Warriors slowly walked to the barricade and prepared themselves for battle, one they knew they could not win, period. I wasn't sure that I could watch the ensuing battle. I knew the Red Stick Warriors would hold their own for a while, but I also knew that the village below would be stormed by General Coffee and his soldiers, and Cherokee and friendly Creeks, after crossing the river in canoes that had been left for escape. When that happened, it would be over for the Creek Warriors who had fought so valiantly. Almost one thousand of them would not return to their homes. I could not watch that, and I was glad Blue Sky Man took my hand, and we left the ill-fated Horseshoe.

Red Eagle surrenders to General Jackson.

Chapter Twenty
Rum With Sharp Knife

We were again on the banks of the Lower Tallapoosa, but this time back at Tuckabatchee. As was the habit of Blue Sky Man, we found ourselves sitting on a log overlooking the slow flowing water. I knew that he would gaze at the river for a while before he began to talk.

"Missy," he said softly. "You know these people were treated bad, very bad. In fact, probably more so than any other race of people. After the big battle at the Horseshoe, those that were left went back to their villages. Many of which had been looted and burned by some of Sharp Knife Jackson's soldiers. I guess you know that several hundred of the women and children were taken prisoner, some by the Cherokee and some by the Lower Creeks that lived on the Chattahoochee. Including Little Flower, her children and her mother." He smiled again, "and of course you know about that. But, Missy, times were sad, so sad. The power of the Creek Nation had been broken never to be the same again. Oh, they did regroup, and I guess were able to be happy again on the remaining land the white man had not yet taken. The white man was not through. In the next twenty years, there would be treaty after treaty taking more of the Creek land." He paused, rubbing his eyes, "ya know Missy, think I must be getting old," he laughed, "I plum forgot to take you to the day that William Weatherford just marched right in to Fort Jackson," he laughed again, "ya know, old Sharp Knife thought so much of himself, he had a new fort built over there were the Coosa and Tallapoosa Rivers join up to form the Alabama and he named it for himself. Would you like to go there, Missy?" Blue Sky Man inquired.

"I sure would Blue Sky Man," I answered.

"Better put your bandanna on this time and do not talk to anyone. Now, the date is August 9, 1814," he said taking my hand again.

Suddenly we were standing just outside Fort Jackson. There seemed to be hundreds of soldiers guarding at least that many Creek, the old, young and the women. Very few warriors were present in the group. They were all quiet and looked wild-eyed and frightened. I knew why when I saw one of the soldiers poke and old man with the butt of his musket. Blue Sky Man said something to a soldier standing guard at the gate. We were immediately allowed to enter.

"Follow me," Blue Sky Man informed me. "Remember, keep quiet and keep your head low. If anyone looks at you."

We went directly to a tent off to the side of the enclosure. A man, his reddish hair ruffled, his shirt unbuttoned, was sitting at a makeshift desk, looking at some tattered papers. Looking up, he grinned, "why Blue Sky Man," he exclaimed as we entered the tent. "How are you my friend?" He glanced at me and just nodded his head with a slight greeting.

Oh, my goodness I thought, I am looking at the horrible man who hated all Indians and who just called Blue Sky Man his friend. Oh my.

"Hello, Andy," Blue Sky Man said warmly. Did he ever have some explaining to do, I thought to myself.

"So, you heard about my victory at the Horseshoe. I think I've taken care of them Creeks." Jackson said with an ugly smirk. "Made some room for the white settlers to move in."

"I guess you did Andy," Blue Sky Man answered sadly.

I noticed that Sharp Knife Jackson was so busy praising himself to realize that Blue Sky Man was not happy over the outcome. Suddenly there was a loud uproar outside and Blue Sky Man and me along with Sharp Knife went outside the tent.

"Kill him, kill him," we heard someone shout.

To my surprise, I saw William Weatherford calmly walk into the camp and asked for General Jackson.

"It's him, its William Weatherford, the Red Eagle. Shoot him," the same person yelled.

I looked to see who wanted to kill William Weatherford on sight. It was Big Warrior from Tuckabatchee. I knew the two men had disagreed but did not realize to what extent.

Blue Sky Man looked at me and said that we should walk away and stand just outside the tent. We did not need to be involved in what was upcoming.

"Yes, I am William Weatherford. I request to see General Jackson," William said calmly after stopping to star at Big Warrior with contempt.

Two soldiers instantly grabbed William's arms.

"I will talk to this man. Let him go," General Jackson said harshly coming out of this tent. The two enemies eyed each other, hatred vivid in the eyes of both men. "How dare you walk into my camp. I should have you hanged." Jackson shouted.

"General Jackson, I do not fear you. You may do what you wish with me. If I still had warriors to fight, I would never stop, but I do not. They are all dead, lying on the battlefield. My reason for coming here today is my people, for the old, the women and the children. They are hiding in the woods, hungry and tired. They have no villages to go home to," he paused, "their homes have been destroyed by the white soldiers. I will bring them in to you if you will give them food and help them."

Despite the hatred he felt for William Weatherford, Jackson admired him for coming into a hostile camp knowing that he could have been shot down. Jackson told him he would help his people but if he ever took up arms again, he would die. The two men on opposing sides talked for a few minutes and surprisingly Jackson invited William Weatherford to join him for supper and a cup or two of rum.

Blue Sky Man whispered to me that we should go. He took my hand and again we were gone.

Chapter Twenty-One
Milly and Barent

Back on the Tallapoosa, and once again sitting by the river, Blue Sky Man asked me what I thought of what had happened between William Weatherford and Andrew Jackson.

"Well," I answered. "That was surprising, but I guess Old Sharp Knife saw the strength and courage in William Weatherford and that he would give his life for his Creek people."

"You know that Jackson sent Bill up to his fancy home in Tennessee? Stayed for nearly a year, he did. So, I reckon too, that maybe they both saw the good in each other. But I tell you I never cared a lick for Old Sharp Knife myself. I just pretended to. Did not trust him no farther than I could spit, and I could spit a long way. Won a spitting contest one time," he laughed, "but that's another story. You heard about a man and a woman named Dubois, right?"

"I have, an amazing story." I answered watching the river flow by me. I was getting as bad Blue Sky Man.

"Want to meet them?" He asked.

"Sure, I would." I answered. I really would like to know if Milly Dubois was the daughter of Big Warrior."

"Then you can ask her yourself. We are really moving on through time. Its around 1828 now. And of course, the white man has taken more of the Creek land, but the area around Tuckabatchee and Talisi are still pretty much in the hands of the Creeks-for now anyway. But let's pay the DuBois family a visit. Come." He invited.

We walked down the riverside path, aways and soon saw the bustling town of Tuckabatchee come into view. It was obvious that the Creek had accepted more of the conveniences of the white man. There were many more cabins as well as livestock. My how things have changed, I thought.

We walked straight over to an extremely nice cabin on the

edge of the village. "This is the DuBois home." Blue Sky Man informed me before calling out. "Hello, anyone home?"

A very pretty, light-skin Creek woman opened the door immediately. "Blue Sky Man," she exclaimed as the two greeted each other with a hug. "Where have you been?" She asked in perfect English. "It seems like such a long time since you were here."

"Hello, Milly," Blue Sky Man answered. "Oh, you know, I've just been traveling around in time," he said, laughing. "This is a new friend of mine. Her name is Missy."

"Why, hello Missy, nice to meet you." The woman said sweetly. "Please come on in. Barent will be back in a little while. It's almost supper time and you know he won't miss that. We're having his favorite and you two will most certainly join us."

"Would Barent's favorite just happen to include apple pie?" Blue Sky Man asked, flashing his big smile again.

"Of course," Milly responded. "Along with beef stew and fresh vegetables."

"Missy, we are in luck today," Blue Sky Man laughed. Just as Milly invited us to sit down in the fabric-covered chairs near the glass pane windows, Barent DuBois entered the front door.

"Blue Sky Man," Barent yelled out. You devil you! Where have you been?" He asked, almost repeating the exact words of his wife.

"Just around in time," Blue Sky Man answered as the two men shook hands in white man fashion and then I was introduced.

"Hello there, if you are a friend of Blue Sky Man, then you are a friend of mine. Welcome to my home." Barent Dubois proclaimed with a slightly different accent.

"Would you like to help me finish up supper and set the table?" Milly asked me.

"Miss Milly, I would be delighted." I said following her to the adjoining kitchen. Just as it had been in an earlier time period with the women, Milly and I quickly became friends and supper was soon ready. I set the table for her using beautiful

Blue Willow China that seemed to be the preferred dishes for more well to do Me`tis women. We talked of the change that had taken place since the battles for the land a few years ago and how some of the whites would never be satisfied until they had it all.

    I knew that Barent was a white man from New York and also an Indian agent to the Creeks and that he had accumulated much land from them, but I did not say anything about that. I also knew that in the future Barent and Milly would acquire more "Creek" land, and he would in fact, become very rich by building grist mills, using the river for power. I also knew that he would build a beautiful larger cabin on the east side of the river just near the falls, but their land holdings would be challenged by the white government. I didn't know who Milly's father was. Judging from her complexion, I could guess, but I wanted to know for sure. So, during a lull in the conversation, I just asked.

    "Miss Milly, I've heard a lot about," I quickly added, "you from Blue Sky Man, but he isn't sure who your father is. So, if you don't mind, could you please tell me? I'm just curious about Blue Sky Man's friends."

    Milly laughed. "No, I don't mind at all. Chief Big Warrior has a daughter and her name is Milly, but I'm not his daughter. My father was a trader by the name of Reed, and I was born down on Okfuskee Creek. That's where I met Barent, and we fell in love," she smiled at her husband.

    "Thank you so much Miss Milly for telling me." I also wanted to know in which cemetery Barent would be buried? The town cemetery, the one in the center of town where both white settlers and Creeks would be buried or a family cemetery. But how would she know what would happen in the future? So, I guess the answer to that will continue be a mystery.

    We enjoyed our delicious meal and conversation with Barent and Milly DuBois, but all too soon Blue Sky Man looked at me and we bid them farewell. Blue Sky Man promised to return, but I knew that I would not.

"Goodbye Miss Milly and Mr. Barent," I said. "It was wonderful to meet you in person." Blue Sky Man looked at me and laughed. He knew he would tell his friends about me next time.

Chapter Twenty-Two
Pole Cat Springs

Blue Sky Man and me walked down the path beside the river. He seemed quiet and pensive, and I wondered what he was thinking. "Blue Sky Man," I asked softly. "Is something wrong?"

He looked at me and smiled. "You know me well, don't you Missy? Yes, the time period we are going to next is sad, very sad. It is the time of removal. The Creek as well as other tribes will experience much suffering and sorrow. Each time I go to this period, I feel their pain and I know you will too."

"I understand and I know that I will feel their sorrow. Where are we going now?" I asked sadly.

"The date is 1836. Ever heard of a place called Pole Cat Springs? A place a mile or so from the Tallapoosa, close to that Federal Road."

"I have," I answered still happy that I could relate to the events and places that he talked about. "Actually, my husband and I were very close to the location a few years," I laughed at the reference to time, "ago. But all we were able to see was a hillside and a valley covered in kudzu."

"Well, what you will soon see will be quite different." Blue Sky Man answered me, his depressed mood becoming lighter. "Missy, Pole Cat Springs"

"Blue Sky Man," I interrupted. "Do you know why the place was called Pole Cat Springs, of all names?"

Blue Sky Man laughed, "well, I don't rightly know Missy. Guess it was because there was a spring where pole cats came to get a drink of water."

"Sound like a likely explanation to me," I said laughing. "Now, please continue."

"Well, a long about 1775 or so, a trader from over Charles Town way came down here to the Tallapoosa. Oh, I know you know all about the traders, but I want to refresh your memory a bit so that you will totally understand. The trader, he brought all those shinny trinkets and things the Creek people liked so well, but it wasn't long before the Creek didn't have much need for such. The men wanted muskets, and the women wanted them pretty blue and white dishes like the white women had. So, the trader just took himself back to Charles Town and got himself a wagon load of the things the Creek people wanted. Built himself a good trading post and took him a pretty Creek woman for his wife. Now, all was well for a while. Then the white people moved in close to the villages. You have already seen what happened then. You know, some of them white folks ain't never satisfied, are they?" He laughed. "Remember, I told you the Talisi and Tuckabatchee people were able to keep their land for a while, but then old Sharp Knife Jackson went and got himself elected president of the whole United States. Then things went from bad to worse and Jackson, he came up with a bill in 1830.

I believe it was called the Indian Removal Act. He got congress to pass in 1834," he paused, "Well, Missy, like I told you them was the saddest days I can remember, and I saw a whole lot of days." Blue Sky Man paused again and rubbed his bright blue eyes, pretending to have dust in them, but I knew he was trying to hide the tears.

"Reckon you wonder, what that has to do with this place, called Pole Cat Springs. So I'll tell you. But first, I want to tell you this so you will completely understand. Come let's walk a litter farther up the path and we will be just outside Pole Cat Springs. It had been decided that all, and I do mean all the Creeks, Cherokee, Choctaw, Chickasaw and any others who considered themselves to be Indians or Native Americans here in the southland would leave their homes and go to the Indian Territory. Course, that would be what now-a-days are the states of Oklahoma and part of Arkansas. You know the Indians had already put up all the fight they could, but that didn't matter none at all. They would go one way or the other. Now, this is what happened many, many times.

Come now, to the home of a Creek family, I think you will want to know what happened to this family. They will not be able to see you this time."

I could see that the family, oh my goodness, it was Soaring Eagle and Little Flower and their children. I watched as…

The family had just sat down for their supper. They were Christian folks and the food was blessed. Then the door was suddenly kicked open and three or four rough, rough looking soldiers burst inside the cabin, one of them pointed his rifle at the horrified family.

"Who are you and what do you want?" Soaring Eagle asked, standing up.

"We want you and your pretty little family here to get your blankets and come with us," with tobaccos juice running from his mouth, he grinned, "now!"

"This is our home," the startled man said, looking at his frightened family.

"Not anymore it ain't," the first soldier replied. "We have orders to take you and all the other," he smirked, "families down to a place called Pole Cat Springs. There's a holding pin for you people. When we bring enough of you in," he laughed. "Then you got a real nice long trip to make to Indian Territory."

Soaring Eagle reached for his musket that was propped against the fireplace. "Wouldn't do that if I was you," another soldier yelled out.

"I said, get your blankets and let's go," the soldier in charge said with anger in his voice.

I watched in horror with tears running down my face as Soaring Eagle looked at Little Flower and the children. "We have no choice; we have to go. We knew this day would come." I continued to watch as the family slowly walked from their home and joined other families on the path down river to face unknown sorrow and pain.

Blue Sky Man took my hand and then we were at Pole Cat Springs. I could not believe what I saw. A barricade made from tall trees had quickly been thrown up to hold the Creek families. There seemed to be no more room for any more people, but more were being pushed inside by gunpoint.

"Blue Sky Man," I whispered. "Can't we stop this? Can't we help them?"

"No, Missy, we cannot, you know that." Blue Sky Man said softly.

"But there is no more room inside. These people are hungry and tired. And just listen to the children crying," I pleaded.

"They will be given food and water a little later and I don't think anymore will be put in this holding pen. But just watch your family and see what happens." Blue Sky Man explained.

As he talked a soldier called out for Soaring Eagle and his family. Then I realized that Soaring Eagle had family ties with the Tuckabatchee Chief and would be released from the holding pen, but they would still leave for Indian Territory with the others when the appointed day came.

We stayed at Pole Cat Springs for a while and at one-point Blue Sky Man had to hold me back. I could not stand to see how these people were being treated.

"Missy, I think we need to move on from here, you are getting too upset." Blue Sky Man whispered.

Suddenly we were in Tuckabatchee. It is late September 1836. There was much activity and preparations were being made. The date of removal had come. I watched as wagons and horses were loaded with the few personal items that could be taken with them. Blue Sky Man pointed at a family headed toward the Tallapoosa. I saw Soaring Eagle gather all his family around him on a little hill that overlooked the river that they loved so much. He began to speak.

"My family, today we will leave this land, the home of the grandmothers. We will go to a new land, and we will make a new home. As long as we have breath in our bodies we will never forget." With tears streaming down his face, Soaring Eagle and his family turned and joined the other Creek people. We stood and watched as they slowly faded away and their Trail of Tears had begun.

Chapter Twenty-Three
Back Home Again

Blue Sky Man touched me on my shoulder. "Ready," he asked me softly. "I think you have had all of the sadness you can bear for now. In fact, our trip in time is almost over. Only a few more brief stops that I want you to see. We are actually going back a few hundred years in time." He smiled, "but I think you will enjoy this and there is one person in particular that I know you will enjoy meeting, and I promise there will be no sadness."

In a flash we were gone and then we were on a hillside overlooking the river. I realized that this river had been the focus point of my trip back into time. I had seen pictures of the scene before me but in no way did they reflect the timeless beauty of what I saw now.

I could hear the wild geese honking as they flew over the shoals of the Tallapoosa River. I understand now why the native people had given the river the name which I knew meant Little Rocks. The shoals stretched for what looked like a half mile or more before tumbling over the great falls. Looking up the river, I saw the islands that in the future would lie hidden beneath the blue waters of the Tallapoosa.

"What do you think of that?" Blue Sky Man asked with excitement in his voice.

"I think this is beautiful. It is much prettier than I imagined it would be. Look, there are the islands." I smiled at Blue Sky Man, "I even know the names. Cat, Buzzard and Long. Is that right?" I asked, pointing at the three islands.

"You are correct," Blue Sky Man answered. "Those are the big ones but there are also several smaller ones scattered across the river."

Looking more closely, I saw movement and I noticed that horses and cows were grazing on two of the larger islands and corn was growing on the other. Amazing, I thought.

"Come, let's go up the river. You know that there have been dams built on this river for a long time. I want you to see the work being done on the first one. We will only be there briefly. Our time is running out," Blue Sky Man stated dejectedly.

I watched with interest as men scurried back and forth guiding mules that pulled big granite rocks that diverted the river flow. It is hard to believe that such remarkable work could be done so long ago.

True to his word. Blue Sky Man had me by the hand and we were gone again and back in town. We stood again on the hillside, this time watching workers use the granite rocks to build a building that was two or three stories high.

"This is 1844 mill that was operated by water power and would later be used to make the carbines for the Confederate Soldiers. I believe you are very interested in that, but again we need to move on." Blue Sky Man said and without changing our position I watched the construction of a long-curved bridge that span the rocks just below where the great falls once were. Martin, Yates and Thurlow Dams had already been built, and I watched as the water slowly flowed down the raceway. I stood mesmerized, knowing that this time passage experience for me would soon be over.

Suddenly I could see images flashing by and realized that we were quickly moving forward in time. I again saw the scene of my childhood, the old cars and short skirts on the girls as they walked down the sidewalk. Then we stopped suddenly. I closed my eyes to stop my head from spinning round and round.

"Oh, I'm so sorry," Blue Sky Man apologized. "I forgot to tell you to close your eyes. Are you alright?"

"Yes, I am now, that was quite a trip." I stated. What comes next? Are we going back again?" Uncertain about what we were going to do.

"Nope, we are staying current." He answered. We are going back down the river a little ways."

"Remember, I told you about meeting one final person,"

Tallassee's Confederate Armory where Carbines were produced during the War Between the States.

Blue Sky Man promised, smiling at me again.

"I do; this must really be a special person. When do I meet him? I asked excited.

"Not a him, but a she. It's a lady, a very special lady," he responded.

"Ready?" He took my hand. "This won't take but a second or two and you won't need to close your eyes."

Quickly we were standing in the middle of a little roadway inside a cotton field. I could feel the heat from the midday sun beating down on my head. I could hear the cheerful song of the redbird and the piercing cry of a red tail hawk high in the blue sky. I realized we were in the vicinity of old Tuckabatchee Town. We walked around a curve and I saw a small, neat cabin-style house. An elderly lady was watering pretty yellow flowers beside the porch. I looked at Blue Sky Man and asked, "Is this the person you wanted me to meet?"

"It is," Blue Sky Man replied. "Come with me."

"Hello," he shouted out.

"Well, I'll be. Hey there Blue Sky Man," she answered. "Where have you been for so long?"

"Aunt Minnie Raintree," Blue Sky Man said happily. "It is so good to see you. Let me give you a hug."

Aunt Minnie Raintree, I thought. How can this be?

Blue Sky Man looked at me over her shoulder and winked. "Aunt Minnie Raintree, I would like for you to meet a good friend of mine. This is Missy, ah, the two of you have a few things in common."

She looked at me and smiled, my what a pretty woman I thought. "Well, hello," she said. "You do look familiar, have we ever met before?"

Blue Sky Man shook his head, I said politely, I don't think so, but it sure is nice to see you, ah, I almost said again, but stopped short. This was amazing. I was completely shocked at what this Blue Sky Man could do and the places he had taken me. Aunt Minnie Raintree took Blue Sky Man and led him to the house.

Alabama Power's Thurlow Dam was built over the 25 foot Tallassee Falls.

"Come on Missy," she smiled. "It is rather warm out here. I have ice tea and just made chocolate chip cookies. I would love for y'all to sit a spell with me. Blue Sky Man, I want to know what you have been up do and where you have gone," she paused and smiled, "this time."

So, she knows that Blue Sky Man is a time traveler, I thought. I wonder what she thinks about me. Does she know? We sat and talked while we enjoyed the ice tea and cookies. They were really as good as the boys had said.

"Oh, Blue Sky Man, let me tell you about my great nephew and his friend." Aunt Minnie Raintree said excitedly. "The old ones came while they were here."

What, I thought. This can not be. We continued to talk and Blue Sky Man looked at me and I knew it was time to go… home, this time. As we stood, Aunt Minnie Raintree reached into the pocket of her pretty blue apron and pulled out a small strand of tiny blue beads, just like the ones that hung from her neck.

"Missy," the lovely old lady said softly. "These are for you. Thank you for the part you played in my life."

She knows, I said to myself. She knows. Aunt Minnie Raintree stood on her tip toes and kissed my cheek. Then Blue Sky Man touched my hand, and we were gone.

****

In only seconds we were back in the upstairs room of the old building. I had already changed back into my jeans and t-shirt. Blue Sky Man had told me to keep the little deer skin pouch filled with the gifts from the past. I rubbed my eyes and shook my head to clear my thoughts. I had just traveled back into time for over a thousand years and had met many important figures in local history and now I was back where I had started. I saw Blue Sky Man standing beside me just as he was before the trip had begun. He smiled his familiar smile.

"Have a good time?" He asked.

"Yes, I did." I replied happily. "I don't understand how this happened, but I will always remember this trip and you."

He stood preparing to leave, "And I will always remember you as well."

"Can I tell anyone about this?" I asked.

"Only your husband. Anyone else would laugh at you, but what you can do is tell others the truth about local history. You do know after all." Blue Sky Man answered.

"Where will you go now?" I asked beginning to feel sad.

"Oh, I think that I will go back to the places and times for a brief stay and then," he laughed his warm, hardy laugh. "Think I just might stay a good, long time with Aunt Minnie Raintree. She is or was a special person, you know."

"Will you come back to the present like you are now?" I questioned. "Will I see you again?"

"No, not like we are talking now, but don't be surprised if you see and old man walking down the street. It might just be me. You will know. Well, Missy, it's been good, but its time now," he smiled, "for me to go back into time."

He kissed my cheek and with that he was gone, and I was alone in the empty room holding the same book in my hand, just as I had been when he entered. I rushed to the window and saw an old man slowly walking down the street. He tipped his old hat and was quickly out of my sight.

What had just happened I wondered. I must have dropped off to sleep and was dreaming. Then I reached inside my jeans pocket and pulled out the little strand of blue beads and saw the pouch. I knew then that what I had experienced was real. I walked down the stairs and saw the owner of the building. He was sitting at his desk just as he had been. Was it only minutes ago or was it a thousand years?

"Did you find what you were looking for?" He asked politely. "You were not up there very long."

"I found exactly what I was looking for and much, much more!" I laughed. "Thank you for allowing me to go upstairs. I really enjoyed myself and did a little time traveling. The man was totally confused. I smiled as I went out the door, turning just in time to see the bright sunlight shinning through —

THE WINDOW OF TIME.

The End

Farm road across a cotton field which was once the sprawling town of Tuckabatchee.

Debra Hughey

Epilogue

It is strange what triggers me to write. From out of nowhere I see or hear something that seems to reach out to me. I hear the words "Write." In this case, there is an old building just down the street from my workplace that I see every day. Just as in the book *Window of Time*, the sun shines in one window and out another. This only happens in one of several windows in the old building. This is what caught my attention.

If you are a local person, then you've probably figured out right away that the story is about our town, Talisi or Tallassee as it is now spelled. As with my other books, the historical information is accurate, but of course, the time travel was my imagination working overtime. I hope you enjoyed reading the book as much as I enjoyed writing it.

— Debra Hughey

Acknowlegements

Photographs by Randall Hughey
Taylor Farms
Alabama Heritage Magazine
Estate of Dovard Taunton
Alabama Power Company
Tallassee Redevelopment Authority
Talisi Historical Preservation Society
A History of Tallassee, Virginia Noble Golden

www.ingramcontent.com/pod-product-compliance
Lightning Source LLC
Chambersburg PA
CBHW070112080526
44586CB00013B/1271